MW00655663

Backstreet Boys

Backstreet Boys

This publication is unauthorized and is not affiliated with the Backstreet Boys or their representatives. Any opinions expressed are solely those of the authors.

Photo Credits: front cover, clockwise from bottom right – James Smeal/Ron Galella LTD. (Brian Littrell), James Smeal/Ron Galella LTD. (Nick Carter), Chris Pizzello/ABC/ImageDirect (Howie Dorough), Ethan Miller/Corbis (AJ McLean) and ReutersNewMedia Inc./Corbis (Kevin Richardson); back cover – Wilberto V.D. Boogaard Sunshine/Retna.

EDITORIAL

Managing Editor: Jeff Mahony
Associate Editors: Melissa A. Bennett, Gia C. Manalio, Mike Micciulla, Paula Stuckart
Assistant Editors: Heather N. Carreiro, Jennifer Renk, Joan C. Wheal
Editorial Assistants: Timothy R. Affleck, Beth Hackett, Christina M. Sette, Steven Shinkaruk

ART

Creative Director: Joe T. Nguyen
Assistant Art Director: Lance Doyle
Senior Graphic Designers: Marla B. Gladstone, Susannah C. Judd, David S. Maloney, Carole Mattia-Slater, David Ten Eyck
Graphic Designers: Jennifer J. Bennett, Sean-Ryan Dudley, Kimberly Eastman, Melani Gonzalez, Jim MacLeod, Jeremy Maendel, Chery-Ann Poudrier

PRODUCTION

Production Manager: Scott Sierakowski

R&D

Product Development Manager: Paul Rasid

ISBN 1-58598-087-0

CHECKERBEE™ and WHO ARE THESE PEOPLE ANYWAY?™ are trademarks of CheckerBee, Inc.
Copyright © 2001 by CheckerBee, Inc.
All rights reserved. No part of this book may be reproduced or transmitted in any form or by any means, electronic or mechanical, including photocopying, recording, or by any information storage or retrieval system, without the written permission of the publisher.

CheckerBee
PUBLISHING

306 Industrial Park Road
Middletown, CT 06457
www.CheckerBee.com

Table Of Contents

Bill Davila/Retna

Who Are These People Anyway?™

Who are AJ, Brian, Howie, Kevin and Nick anyway? Why, they're the members of the Backstreet Boys, of course. One of today's hottest bands, the Backstreet Boys have been winning over people of all ages and backgrounds with their irresistible hip-hop and soft, soulful ballads.

This guide will take you behind-the-scenes to give you the REAL scoop on each of the band members. Why is AJ's nickname "Bone?" What does Brian say are his biggest influences? What pranks does Nick like to pull on his fellow Backstreet Boys? You'll find the answers to all of these questions and more in the profiles for the band members, each of which include full-color photos, little-known facts and quotes from the guys themselves!

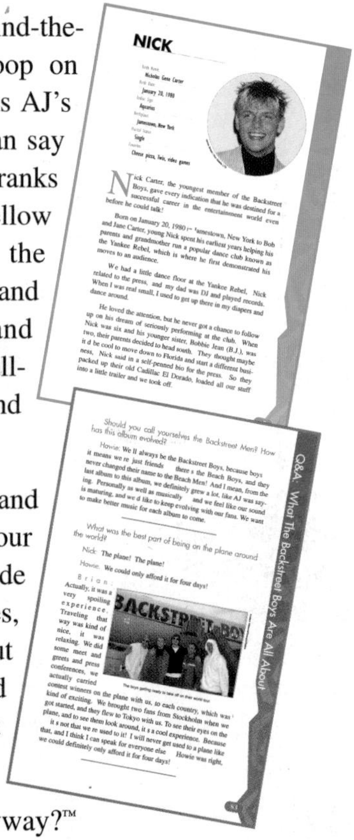

NICK

Nicholas Gene Carter

January 20, 1980

Aquarius

Jamestown, New York

Single

Cheese pizza, Twix, video games

Nick Carter, the youngest member of the Backstreet Boys, gave every indication that he was destined for a successful career in the entertainment world even before he could talk!

Born on January 20, 1980 i~ 'amestown, New York to Bob and Jane Carter, young Nick spent his earliest years helping his parents and grandmother run a popular dance club known as the Yankee Rebel, which is where he first demonstrated his moves to an audience.

We had a little dance floor at the Yankee Rebel, Nick related to the press, and my dad was DJ and played records. When I was real small, I used to get up there in my diapers and dance around.

He loved the attention, but he never got a chance to follow up on his dream of seriously performing at the club. When Nick was six and his younger sister, Bobbie Jean (B.J.), was two, their parents decided to head south. They thought maybe it d be cool to move down to Florida and start a different business, Nick said in a self-penned bio for the press. So they packed up their old Cadillac El Dorado, loaded all our stuff into a little trailer and we took off.

Q&A: What The Backstreet Boys Are All About

Should you call yourselves the Backstreet Men? How has this album evolved?

Howie: We ll always be the Backstreet Boys, because boys it means we re just friends there s the Beach Boys, and they never changed their name to the Beach Men! And I mean, from the last album to this album, we definitely grew a lot, like AJ was saying. Personally as well as musically and we feel like our sound is maturing, and we d like to keep evolving with our fans. We want to make better music for each album to come.

What was the best part of being on the plane around the world?

Nick: The plane! The plane!

Howie: We could only afford it for four days!

Brian: Actually, it was a very spoiling experience. Traveling that way was kind of nice, it was relaxing. We did some meet and greets and press conferences, we actually carried contest winners on the plane with us, to each country, which was kind of exciting. We brought two fans from Stockholm when we got started, and they flew to Tokyo with us. To see their eyes on the plane, and to see them look around, it s a cool experience. Because it s not that we re used to it! I will never get used to a plane like that, and I think I can speak for everyone else Howie was right, we could definitely only afford it for four days!

You'll also find out how the band got started, what it's like to be on tour with the Backstreet Boys and a guide to all of the band's TV appearances, awards and videos. Plus, find out how long your favorite songs stayed on top of the music charts and what the critics thought of them!

The Who Are These People Anyway?™ series brings today's top celebrities right into your living room. Check out our guides on 'NSYNC, pop music stars, movie stars and TV stars for more information on your favorite celebrities! And check out our web site at *www.checkerbee.com* for more details about the series that really sizzles! ♪

The Backstreet Boys' Rise To Fame

A rebel is described by dictionaries as "one who fights against, resists or refuses allegiance to established authority." According to that definition, the Backstreet Boys are true rebels, for when they started their singing careers, they resisted the popular sound in the music industry, choosing instead to go their own way. As a result, the group was dismissed early on by record executives and other insiders who said they'd never make it onto the charts.

The Backstreet Boys Come Together

The band's roots were planted in Orlando, Florida, in 1992, where teenagers AJ McLean, Nick Carter and Howie Dorough were trying to score acting gigs when they weren't in school. "AJ and I met at a talent contest," Howie told *Hello* magazine. "And we ran into Nick at various auditions."

Their success as actors had been limited. Howie landed a few insubstantial roles in feature films and AJ had just auditioned for Disney's *Mickey Mouse Club* TV show. Unlike soon-to-be stars Keri Russell and Justin Timberlake, though, he didn't make the cut.

Howie sports a flashy look for the camera.

Larry Busacca/Retna

So AJ, Howie and Nick decided to join forces and start a singing act. At first, like their acting efforts, they didn't get much attention. After all, they were hopelessly behind the times – at least that's what the music industry thought. The soon-to-be Backstreet Boys were unabashed pop singers, which was decidedly uncool in the early 1990s. Alternative music was the thing – grunge rock groups like Nirvana were hot, while cheerful popsters like New Kids On The Block were being dropped by their labels.

B. Khan/Retna

Who is this blond-haired cutie? Why, it's Nick!

In an interview with the *Chicago Tribune,* Vincent DeGiorgio of RCA Records said about the situation, "Let's face it, if you turned on MTV at that time, you were seeing a lot of hip-hop artists and the latest alternative superstars."

Answering An Ad

Who you weren't seeing were pop singers like AJ, Howie and Nick. But the trio didn't care about what was "in" at the moment and believed in the power of their music. They loved soulful pop music and they were determined to bring it back into style. So the three teens continued plugging away, rehearsing at their homes and performing occasionally at local street fairs and any other venue that would have them. After a few months, they attracted the attention of Trans Continental Airline magnate Louis J. Pearlman, who recognized that these talented young boys were onto something.

Naming The Band

The Backstreet Boys were named after the parking lot at Orlando's Backstreet Market, where friends would "just hang out and chill." "Boys" was added to symbolize the guys' friendship with each other. ♪

Pearlman desperately wanted to get a foothold in the music industry, believing with all his heart that boy groups could still work despite the current musical climate. To this end, he hooked up with former New Kids road managers Johnny and Donna Wright. Together they took a classified ad out in the *Orlando Sentinel* in June of 1992 that read, "Teen male vocalists: producer seeks male teen singers that move well between 16-19 years of age. Wanted for New Kids–type singing-dance group. Send photo or bio of any kind to . . . "

Did You Know . . .

. . . that 'NSYNC band member Chris Kirkpatrick used to wait on the Backstreet Boys at an Outback Steakhouse. A fan of the Backstreet Boys, he used to tell the boys he wanted to be just like them! ♪

"We heard of a man named Lou Pearlman who was starting a label called Trans Continental Records," Howie has said of how the guys hooked up with their first manager. "And he was looking for talent. We were harmonizing, so we went in and auditioned for him. He suggested that we extend the group to five members."

This suggestion resulted in Kevin Richardson, an employee at Orlando's Disney World (he played Aladdin), auditioning for the group in March of 1993. A month later, Kevin, in turn, brought in his cousin from Kentucky, Brian Littrell. With the group now complete, they chose a name: Backstreet Boys, which was derived from a local hangout. "Actually, it was called the

Bob Berg/Retna

Who can resist this handsome group?

Backstreet Market," Kevin told the press. "It was just a local hangout. It was a flea market, but when there was no flea market going on, it was a big parking lot. That was where the kids would drive their cars, hang out in their convertibles and listen to music. That's how we got 'Backstreet.' We put 'Boys' on it, because no matter how old we get, we feel we'll always be boys."

Larry Busacca/Retna

The Backstreet Boys kick off the release of their 1997 debut album with a performance in New York City's Virgin megastore.

What they also were, was a success. In fact, Donna Wright admitted to *Billboard* magazine that she initially had misgivings about signing the group. "I wasn't sure if we wanted to get involved with them," she said. "The New Kids had just finished up two years prior and pop seemed to be over. But hearing them sing just gave me chills running from the back of my heels to the top of my head. I really felt like we had something there."

Hitting The Road

So Donna Wright swallowed her concerns and took a gamble on the group. After she and husband Johnny – as well as Lou Pearlman – signed each of the Backstreet Boys to exclusive contracts, they set their sights on getting the Backstreet Boys a recording contract, which was no easy task. Explained Howie, "We'd go to local labels and sing a cappella in their foyers. We'd sing anywhere, for anybody."

"We're not perfect. We're just a bunch of regular Joes that just want to do something that they love . . . . If they want to look at us as being teen idols, it's cool."
— AJ on the group's teen-idol status.

Unfortunately, those early efforts didn't do very much good. What Pearlman and the Wrights discovered was that the best way to secure a record contract was to gain visibility for the group; to build a fan base so that record companies would feel secure that someone out there would buy the album. They set about achieving this goal by booking the guys for live performances anywhere they could, ranging from private parties to high school pep rallies. Since many of their shows were during the day, AJ and Nick, the last remaining Backstreet Boys still in high school, were forced to give up attending classes in favor of tutors.

"Those [early performances] were the hardest," Kevin looked back in an interview. "You could tell the [kids] were thinking, 'What is this, the second coming of New Kids On The Block?' But once we started showing them we could really sing, we won them over every time."

larry Busacca/Retna

The Boys ham it up for the camera at New York City's All Star Cafe in 1997.

But it was slow going. Gigs were hard to come by and most of them were at very small venues. Mercury Records nearly signed them to a contract in the fall of 1993, but the deal fell through at the last minute. After all this time of performing at malls and schools, and staying at cheap motels, the Backstreet Boys were beginning to wonder if they were ever going to get their big break.

Patrick Ford/Retna

Brian, Nick, AJ, Kevin and Howie (left to right) at the 1996 MTV Europe Music Awards.

That break did come, of course, but from an unexpected source. In 1994, the Backstreet Boys were hired to perform at events across the country for the Students Against Drunk Driving (SADD) awareness campaign. As Kevin told the press, "Being on the SADD tour before we even had a record deal really helped get our confidence up."

It also gave them that elusive record deal. It was during one SADD performance that they caught the attention of Jive Records' Dave McPherson and Jeffrey Fenster. "The first time I saw them was at a SADD function in Columbus, Ohio," Fenster explained, "at the convention center in front of a pretty big group of junior high and high school students who had never seen them before. They performed great, did some original material, sang some a cappella. They were a very polished unit when we signed them. Even though they were not completely self-contained artists in terms of writing and producing their own material, they were very much a unit that worked extremely well together."

David Tonge/Retna

Up close and personal with the Backstreet Boys!

The Big Time: In Europe

McPherson and Fenster auditioned the group and, impressed by their vocal abilities and attractive personalities, decided to give them a shot. Shortly after signing with Jive in 1995, the Backstreet Boys recorded the single "We've Got It Goin' On," which was released simultaneously in the United States and England that August. The single didn't do much business in either country, resulting in the cancellation of a planned mini-tour of the United States to promote it. However, a pleasant surprise came from

Germany in October when the song made it to that country's top 10, eventually earning the group their first gold record.

That heat continued to intensify between November and December when they toured the United Kingdom with the Smash Hits Roadshow. During the winter of 1996, they began a tour of Europe, focusing heavily on Germany. Kids in Europe reacted enthusiastically to the Backstreet Boys and their music. As a result, "Get Down" was released as a single in the spring and reached #14 on the U.K. charts.

Chris V.D. Vooren/Sunshine/Retna

Nick jokes around during a quiet moment in Amsterdam.

In April 1996, the Backstreet Boys released their first album, and in country after country in the European community, it went gold and platinum. By the end of 1996, they were clearly on their way. The U.K.'s *Smash Hits* magazine even honored the Backstreet Boys as "Newcomers Of The Year."

Three Cheers For The Backstreet Boys!

Jive, the Backstreet Boys' original record label, helped promote the band in the United States by sending samplers of the Backstreet Boys' music to summer cheerleader camps, teen girl organizations and subscribers to the Sweet Valley High book series. ♪

Their popularity in Europe quickly spread. "Over there," Brian said during a press conference, "they had a bunch of what's called 'boy groups,' so we had a ready-made market. But since we were Americans, we were a fresh new sound for Europe. We had more of an edge, and unlike a lot of other boy groups, we were more than just a bunch of pretty guys. We could sing."

Howie added, "It just blew up over there. America wasn't ready for a group like us. And over in Europe, they were just more accepting. We came over with a very fresh, Americanized sound. They just embraced us with open arms. I think it was because we had a really fresh sound. We came across over there doing a lot of a cappella music in the beginning, which was something kind of new for them."

Larry Busacca/Retna

The Boys don their sports jerseys for this 1997 photo.

Soon enough, the European Backstreet Boys craze was underway. Said Howie in *US* magazine, "We had some crazy things start to happen in Europe, like fans stowing away on the bus, girls climbing over barbed-wire fences and showing up in our dressing rooms with their skirts cut up." To *Teen* magazine, he added, "We used to talk to fans in the hotel lobby, but we can't be as personable with them anymore because the hype is so big over there."

Krystal Clear

The Backstreet Boys recently started a record label of their own. They just signed their first act, a talented female artist named Krystal. ♪

With their success on a sharp upswing, they released a second single, "I'll Never Break Your Heart," which quickly surpassed its predecessor. The song went gold in Germany and hit #1 in Austria. The group was voted the "Number One International Group" by German TV viewers.

Shortly thereafter, the Backstreet Boys had entered the radio and video rotation in Canada, and their incredible forward momentum was unstoppable. Country after country fell to the Backstreet Boys, fueled by their non-stop touring, a third single, "Get Down (You're the One For Me)," and the release of their self-titled international debut album. By the fall of 1996, they'd taken over the charts in Asia and Australia and were met by screaming fans everywhere they went.

Yet despite this success, the United States still seemed like a distant dream. "A lot of people are skeptical about us," Nick told *Teen* at the time. "We want to show our country what we can do."

"It was kinda strange at first," Kevin related to *Hello* magazine. "Our popularity in Europe was so big and the number of fans was amazing. Our success started there. We would leave Europe and have a couple of hundred fans at the airport. Then we would come home to the U.S. and no one knew us."

Simon Ritter/Retna

The energy during a Backstreet Boys concert is undeniable!

Despite the stubborn anonymity they faced in their homeland, the Backstreet Boys were determined to crack the U.S. market. They began 1997 by making U.S. television appearances on programs such as *Saturday Night Live* and eventually performed atop one of the Macy's Thanksgiving Day floats. In between, they issued "Quit Playin' Games (With My Heart)" in the United States and then their U.S. debut album. This time, their homeland was ready for the Backstreet Boys. A U.S. tour settled the matter once and for all. The guys found themselves headlining sold-out concerts across the country.

"We're not trying to make a statement with our music. We're just trying to make good music that makes people want to sing along, forget their problems for a minute."

— Kevin on the Backstreet Boys' music ♪

Why did the Backstreet Boys finally click in the United States? Teens in the United States had no singing groups they could call their own. Girls didn't think much of mean-spirited rap songs that were popular at the time, and the mechanized dance sound of the early 1990s was dying quickly. So there was large community of music lovers was waiting for the kind of up-tempo dance grooves and soulful ballads that BSB specialized in.

A Lot Of Hard Work

After a year of living their American dream, the Backstreet Boys were suddenly faced with competition. Their success helped usher grunge and electronica into the dustbin of music history and

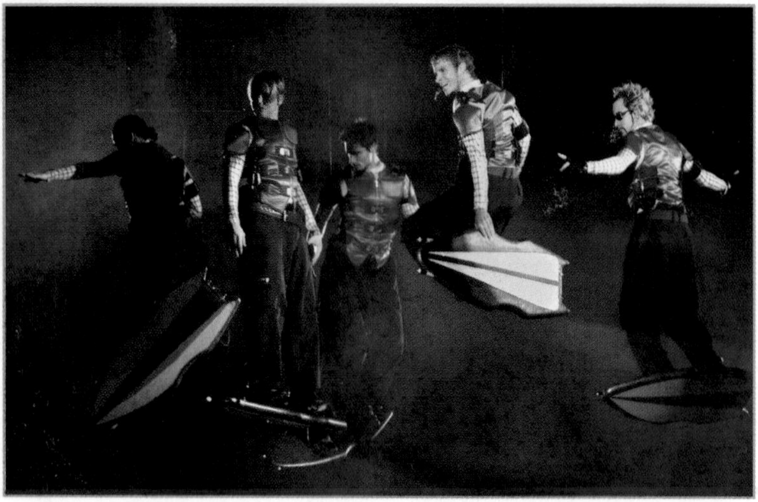

AP/WWP

The band soars through the air at the start of their 1999 concert in Frankfurt, Germany.

triggered a wave of Backstreet Boys–like groups, from Hanson to 'NSYNC. The guys, however, just felt good that the hard work had finally paid off.

Robert Durrell/L.A. Times/Retna

From left, Kevin, Nick, AJ, Brian and Howie show they are not only great singers – they are great dressers too!

"Two years of practice six days a week, small tours of schools around the States, and then, after we signed with Jive, there was three years of touring," Howie has said of the group's long trek to fame. "People have this misconception that we do a show, go shopping, lie by a pool and go do the next show. But we haven't lived that life yet. Mostly, when everyone else is at the after-concert party, we're on our way to the next gig, getting there with barely enough time to shower and rehearse before going on."

In spite of their amazing success, the guys seem to have remained down to earth. In *Hello* magazine, Howie said that the group's ability to deal with their success has much to do with their families. "We all come from middle-class backgrounds," he explained. "Hard-working, wholesome people. We've all worked very hard to get where we are today and we appreciate very much what we have. We never take anything for granted." ♪

AJ

Robert Spencer / Retna

AJ

Birth Name:
Alexander James McLean

Birth Date:
January 9, 1978

Zodiac Sign
Capricorn

Birthplace
West Palm Beach, Florida

Marital Status
Single

Favorites
Poetry, drawing cartoons

Although the Backstreet Boys are every girl's dream, that doesn't mean all of them are perfect enough to take home to mom and dad.

That's because there's a wild side to the Backstreet Boys – and he's AJ McLean, the multi-tattooed member of the group. Fans love the unpredictable AJ, but the group's managers weren't always so sure he'd be a hit.

"One of our managers told me off when I got my tattoo," he told *Smash Hits* magazine. "They were all angry with me. I just thought, 'So what?' They were afraid it was gonna kind of affect our image, but we're not about an image. We're about good music. So what I do to my body is my business. It's forever, so I have to be prepared."

A Wild And Crazy Guy

And AJ, more than most pop stars, is prepared for controversy. In fact, he meets it head-on, giving the supermarket tabloids a run for their money with tales of his outlandish behavior. And AJ himself has admitted that he has a tendency to stretch the truth, just for the fun of it. "I'm really good at it," he admitted. "I stopped, though, because I was getting a little carried away. Things started getting back around to me, and you're not a good liar if you get caught."

Still think your parents wouldn't mind having him over for dinner? What if he insisted they call him by his nickname "Bone?" How would they feel about that?

Theodore Wood / CP / Retna

AJ sports a colorful new look for the 2000 MTV Awards in Stockholm.

What the heck does "Bone" mean, anyway? "There are three interpretations" of the nickname, he told a reporter. "One is the rude one; one is the way that I look, being so skinny; and one has to do with a bunch of beads I used to wear – they look like bones. Sometimes I won't even answer to AJ, I'll only answer to Bone."

"I didn't hang out with the cool people. I was kinda quiet and by myself. I got pretty good grades, too. Except once I got an F for pre-algebra. I hate math."

— AJ on school. ♪

As is pretty obvious, Alexander James McLean marches to his own drummer, which is probably why he is so enormously popular with the fans of the Backstreet Boys.

AJ's Adjustment

AJ was born on January 9, 1978, at Palm Beach, Florida's Bethesda Memorial Hospital, the only child of Robert and Denise, employees of IBM and a local hotel, respectively. Although he's often stated that he had a wonderful childhood, he admits it wasn't all singing and dancing.

When AJ was only 4 years old, his parents divorced. The breakup was not amicable, and AJ's father disappeared from his life. The separation from his father was difficult for AJ, who felt he lost out on all of the father-son activities most of his friends had. This may have contributed to his wild streak, but rebellion came so naturally to AJ that he's not too sure. What he does know for sure is that he really missed his father.

"I saw my father for about two days at Christmas time when I was 6. That was it. I never saw him again," he told *Teen* magazine. That finally changed when he discovered, at the age of 18, that his father was living only a short distance away from him.

Deciding to take matters into his own hands, he paid his father a surprise visit. "This guy opens the door and I'm like, 'Is there a Robert McLean home?' He said, 'Alex?' I was like, 'Whoa, Dad, you recognize me?' I walked in and there's Backstreet Boys stuff everywhere. He'd been keeping up with me since the day I started."

Who is that innocent-looking boy? It's AJ!

Mark Cairns / Retna

Another major adjustment in AJ's life occurred when he transferred from a performing-arts school to a regular school. It was rough going, and he found that regular school wasn't as much fun – especially the social part. "I didn't hang out with the cool people," he said in an interview. "I was kinda quiet and by myself. I was Mr. Comedian when I was with my own friends, but otherwise I was mostly quiet. I got pretty good grades, too.

Except once I got an F for pre-algebra. I hate math."

AJ takes to the stage in New York City.
Melanie Edwards / Retna

To *Smash Hits* magazine he admitted, "In school, everyone was afraid of me cuz I was such a freak. No one would come near me; they were like, 'What the hell's wrong with him? He's so weird.' I didn't fit in. I was in a class of my own. I was just very different. I was an entertainer. High school is all about basketball, football, fights, gangs, this and that. If you're a singer or dancer, then you're considered a freak. But just look at me now."

AJ And The Arts

"I was nervous. All my friends and family were watching as I walked up the steps of the stage to accept my diploma. And what do I do? I trip!"

— AJ on his high school graduation.

AJ's family has always supported him unconditionally, and he cites his grandparents, his Uncle Bill, Aunt Darlene and his cousin Kathy for their kind words. They also gave him the encouragement to pursue his passion for the arts, which he started doing even before he was old enough to go to school.

"Actually," he told *16,* "I wanted acting to be my

first career. I wanted to be a dancer or an actor." To *Teen Beat* he said, "I was also modeling for print work in JC Penney and national magazines. Like, if they showed a picture of a family in an ad, I would be one of the little kids."

Of all his family members, though, the most supportive was his mother, who, in the early days of the Backstreet Boys, accompanied the band with the underaged AJ. She made sure he kept up with his studies and, when the group wasn't achieving the kind of success they were looking for, she wouldn't let him give up on his dream.

Bill Davila / Retna

AJ catches a quick break – wonder what he's thinking about?

Along with the acting, dancing and singing, AJ also allowed his imagination to take him in a different direction. He has loved puppets since he was a little kid, and so he became a puppeteer, using many of the stuffed animals he had since he was a baby to put on shows for people. "I was bored," he told the press. "I used to have a lot of plush toys and I'd play with the plush toys, and I got into puppets. I did a lot of talent shows with puppets. It just caught on because no one had seen anyone my age be that interested and having that much fun doing stuff with puppets. I got a major kick out of it, and I still do."

Despite his success as a puppeteer, it was acting that he was most passionate about. He made his semi-professional acting debut at the Royal Palm Dinner Theater in Florida, playing Dopey in a production of *Snow White And The Seven Dwarves.* Many other acting jobs followed – by the time he was 12, he had done more than two dozen plays.

AJ sends his greetings from Amsterdam.

C. Vooren / Retna

It was at that time that AJ was accepted into a well-regarded performing-arts school near his home. The dance classes at the school gave him the skills to not just mimic what he saw from other performers, as he had done in the past, but to actually understand the craft behind the movements.

"If you come to one of our shows, we have anywhere from 15- to 65-year-olds. I don't know any other 'teeny bopper band' that brings entire families [to concerts]."
— AJ on the band's wide-ranging popularity.

The acting classes paid off, too. He landed a few roles, most notably on the Nickelodeon-produced series *Hi, Honey, I'm Home; Welcome Freshmen;* and *Fifteen.*

Despite all of AJ's success, he missed out on many of the things that kids take for granted. "I never went to my prom," he said in an interview. "I never really went to high school. I got tutored. I graduated, but I did my class work in my hotel room. I still got to fly back home and graduate with my class, though. I was nervous. All my friends and family were watching as I walked up the steps of the stage to accept my diploma. And what do I do? I trip!"

AJ's Alter Ego

That was one of the only missteps of his career; a career that has allowed him a great deal of creative freedom. In fact, not long ago, AJ basically changed his identity, not only to allow him to try a different kind of music but to help VH1's Save the Music Foundation. To this end, he created a new persona for himself, the R&B/rock-inspired "Johnny No-Name." AJ has taken Johnny out on the road, performing to crowds and experiencing great success. Johnny's pretty different from AJ, though – most notably in the fact that he is British and from Nashville, Tennessee.

"He's on constant probation," AJ told *SonicNet* about Johnny. "Every time he does a solo show, he gets off his probation, and then at the end of the show, he has to go back to jail. I don't know what he does, but he's always in trouble. I'm not. I'm a little angel."

Jim Smeal / Ron Galella LTD.

AJ (in white) and the rest of the band pose for photos at the 41st Annual Grammy Awards in 1999.

AJ has written songs for Johnny. One of them, "Privacy Homicide," is about AJ's loss of privacy. "I do love the attention," he has said, "but then there are certain cases where I can't stand it. Like when I'm trying to eat dinner with my family but I don't want people to think I'm a [jerk] because I won't sign an autograph."

This alter-ego's original name was Johnny Suede. The inspiration for that name came from a label on a jacket that read, "Johnny Suede Dressed To Pimp." AJ used the name until a writer/director named Tom DiCillo threatened to sue because he had made a film starring Brad Pitt under that name.

AJ pours his heart out into the microphone.

Dave Hogan / ImageDirect

Naturally, the real difference between Johnny and the Backstreet Boys is in the form of the music. Explained AJ, "Me and a couple of guys in the band have sat down and tried to work out some original Johnny No-Name music with more of a rock-alternative edge and a hip-hop–type vibe. Johnny's music is a wide range of every genre of music that I grew up listening to that has had some influence on me." At the Hard Rock Cafe he added, "I'm not really blind-sided to one specific type of music. I listen to everything. Rock, to me, is more free than pop. Pop is more giddy and happy. Rock and roll has been around for ages and will never die. Johnny is gonna do more of the rock thing."

The real question, of course, is what the other members of Backstreet Boys think of all this. "I know," he said, "that they actually want to sit in the audience and watch me perform, which is kind of weird." Possibly even weirder is that fellow

Backstreet Boy Howie Dorough has occasionally joined him on stage, which might take away from AJ's efforts to establish an identity apart from the world-famous quintet.

"It's still songs for everyone. Of every race, color and age. We're thinking more now than we ever used to. We're all a little bit more grown up."
— AJ on the direction the band's music is taking.

"I want people to differentiate Johnny from AJ," he told the *Minneapolis Star Tribune.* "It's frustrating to be on stage and still be looked at as so-and-so from the Backstreet Boys." Being stereotyped as a boy band is something that has grown very tiresome for him.

"When we first started out," he related in a radio interview, "when we released the very first Backstreet Boys album in the U.S., it was kind of inevitable. I mean, we really had nowhere to go to hide. We couldn't hide underneath a chair or something and just say, you know, we're not going to take it and kinda run away. We always dealt with it head-on and, basically, it's gonna happen. It still happens to this day, even though we've gained a lot

Bill Davila / Retna

The Backstreet Boys (AJ is on the left) make an appearance outside the VH1 Men Strike Back concert.

more respect over the last two years. And it's going to continue to happen just because of our image and because you have five white guys singing pop music, and our main market seems to be 15- to 25-year-olds. But yet, what people don't realize is, if you come to one of our shows, we have anywhere from 15-to-65-year-olds. I don't know any other 'teeny bopper band' that brings entire families, and, you know, dads say how much they listen to our music and stuff like that. That really makes us feel good."

Dave Hogan / ImageDirect

Brian (left) and AJ (right) wait for their cue at a rehearsal.

Of course, fame does have its downside. "Touring can be exhausting sometimes," he said. "And sometimes there are just too many demands made on us."

But such things, he emphasizes, are minor complaints, considering all that he has to be thankful for.

"The fact that things are going so quickly is blowing my mind," he said. "The pace of success – it's like, 'Slow down and give me a little time to have a life.'"

Are You AJ's Type?

AJ says that he's looking for a girl with beautiful eyes and long fingernails, who has a great personality and a terrific sense of humor.

Gaining Perspective

Yet despite the classification as a boy band, AJ believes that the Backstreet Boys have all grown a lot, with a lot of the credit for that going to Brian Littrell's open-heart surgery.

"After Brian's surgery," he told *Tiger Beat,* "we all kind of took a little time to really grow up. Brian especially made a comment to me that he's really grown up between the time that he had the surgery and now, and I think all of us have taken the opportunity to really look at this and see that it can happen to anybody. It doesn't matter how old you are. And it's not a bad thing or a good thing. I think everything happens for a reason. And it was bound to happen one day or another."

AJ listens carefully at a press conference.

Henry Lamb / Ron Galella LTD.

Reality has had a real effect on their lives, and has influenced each member of the band in a variety of ways, including the way that they write songs. AJ believes that they've managed to attain a more adult level of songwriting than they ever could have before. "It's still songs for everyone," he said, "of every race, color and age, but it's just that we're thinking more now than we ever used to; to not just write a song about, 'Let's go have a party and have a good time.' We're all a little bit more grown up."

And their fans are all growing up right along with them.

BRIAN

John Gladwin / Retna

BRIAN

Birth Name
Brian Thomas Littrell
Birth Date
February 20, 1975
Zodiac Sign
Pisces
Birthplace:
Lexington, Kentucky
Marital Status
Married to Leighanne Wallace
Favorites
Mac and cheese, Jodeci

James Smeal / Ron Galella LTD

What is Brian Littrell looking for in life? "To be a singer, to do something I love; to go to work every day to do something I enjoy. And to have a talent that you can use, and actually use it. I think it's destiny why we're all here together."

Needless to say, Brian is not what one would expect from a member of one of today's hottest phenomenons, the Backstreet Boys. In a time when stardom seems to go hand-in-hand with ego and a certain level of self-destructiveness, the Backstreet Boys, and Brian in particular, seem to have risen above the fray via a certain degree of – if you'll excuse the language – wholesomeness.

Choir Boy

"As a young boy," he explained in a self-penned bio that was distributed to the press, "I ate, drank and slept church whether I liked it or not. I'd rather be playing on Sundays, but it grew on me and I think it had a lot to do with the way I live my life now."

Born on February 20, 1975, in Lexington, Kentucky, Brian was greeted by his father, Harold, mother, Jackie, and 3-year-old brother, Harold III. Although he had a fairly normal childhood, by kindergarten he had a sense that singing would play a major role in his life. "My mom and dad both sing like birds, so they would sing in church all the time," he said in that same press bio. "I was always involved in the children's chorus at church, and I was always singing up on stage." He performed his first "solo" at the tender age of 6 in front of the 1,500-member congregation, and seemed on his way – in a matter of speaking.

Wilberto Boogaard Sunshine / Retna

Brian takes a moment out of his busy schedule to pose for the camera.

Brian Survives A Health Scare

The following year, however, things turned considerably darker for him. A childhood injury resulted in an infection that spread through his blood and literally threatened his life, simultaneously causing doctors to discover a murmur and a pinprick-sized hole in his heart. Things had gotten so bad, in fact, that Brian's parents were told to make funeral arrangements – the infection had spread too far and too quickly for much to be done.

"I'll never forget something that my mom said when I was 10 or 11," he reflected. "'You know, Brian, when you were in the hospital, I was holding on to you for dear life, because I wanted to keep you here with me so bad . . . you're my baby and I needed you. I finally realized that God has different needs.' She realized that I was a blessing in her life, and she had to let me go if it was my time. That night when she made that prayer, she gave me up. She said, 'Whatever happens, happens; if it's meant to be.' And from then on, I started slowly to get better and recover."

In the pages of *Tiger Beat* he added, "I was in the hospital for a month and a half of my first-grade year, so I missed all of school. I remember that I returned from the hospital and there was a bicycle there waiting for me in front of the house – a yellow and red bicycle with a big banana seat on it. This was 1980, and it's still my favorite bike of all time."

Family Comes First

Brian recently spent a lot of time in Nashville helping to produce his brother Harold's country album. ♪

Physician predictions that he would spend his life as an invalid also proved to be erroneous. Brian felt much better than he had, but his parents were extremely protective until he started growing and was proving himself stronger. "Our church was fairly large and they had a whole football field," he said. "Every summer they had a little soccer camp for kids my age and a little bit younger, and I would always try to get out there and play with them. My heart being weak at the time, my parents were scared. They never let me play soccer, so I eventually picked up a basketball and I played for the church league with all my high school buddies.

Brian interacts with the audience during a concert.

Simon Ritter / Retna

Brian shows his talent goes beyond music.

"In basketball, you do as much running as in soccer. It's crazy. Ever since then, I really got into it and I never had any problems. A couple of years after I got out of the hospital, I was growing and my parents slowly let me do what I wanted to do."

The Acting Bug

What he wanted to do, as he ultimately discovered, was continue to perform, moving beyond the church altar. He began appearing in school plays, among them *Grease,* and honed his singing skills while being mentored by his music teacher, Barry Turner, who, as he has said, "got to mold me." It all came to a head in his junior year of high school when he sang the spiritual song "Another Time, Another Place" in a school talent show. The response from the audience (particularly the young ladies in attendance) absolutely convinced him that singing was what he wanted to do with his life.

> **Best Friends Through Thick And Thin**
>
> In July of 2000, Brian's two chihuahuas, Litty Leigh and Tyk Thomas, were dognapped by two women. They were recovered, unharmed, by police four days later. ♪

"In church," he reflected, "it was, 'Man, you're good, you have a really nice voice,' and that was pretty much it. I would get compliments like that, but it never really set in. I always knew I wanted to sing, but I never really took it seriously until my junior year of high school.

[Before the talent show] I had just gotten out of my chorus class earlier in the day and I was a nobody. But yet, when I stepped up on stage and got behind those lights, it was totally different. I was just an instant star. I think that was the point in my life when I knew that if I could pull something off like that with my peers, then there definitely had to be people out in the world who would like it as well. And from then on, it was such a rush."

Mick Hutson / Retna

Brian performing in 1995.

Brian's original plan was to continue using his talent and developing it even further in college. "I was very close to graduating high school," he told journalist Angie Nichols. "I was offered a singing scholarship to the University of Cincinnati Bible College. I was going to go to Cincinnati, which is only 100 miles from Lexington, so I would be close to home, yet away from home."

The Backstreet Boys

Unbeknownst to Brian, while he sat in his high school history class, his life was about to be altered in a startling way. As it turns out, his cousin, Kevin Richardson, had become part of a fledgling Orlando, Florida–based pop band called the Backstreet Boys, and the group was in search of a new member. Kevin turned to Brian.

"When we would have family outings, Kevin would always go hang out with my brother," he said. "It was like my brother and him were real tight, because they were the same age. I was the baby of the family. My brother sings also, but he doesn't really sing pop/R&B-style the way we have. He likes heavy metal, rock 'n' roll. They would get together and sing and pretend they were rock stars, and my brother would beat on the drums. My brother never took it seriously like I didn't take it seriously – until I was just thrown into it.

Bill Davila / Retna

Brian films a commercial in 1999 for Sears, a sponsor of the Backstreet Boys tour.

"Everyone knows about the day Kevin called me from Orlando for the Backstreet Boys. I was sitting in my U.S. History class, it was the last class of the day, sixth hour, and it was April, 1993. So I get home and right when I walk in the door, I'm like, 'Mom, I gotta tell ya, I gotta tell ya,' and she was like, 'Yeah, Kevin called about the group and told me all about it.'"

Being a practical mom, Jackie was more concerned about her son's continuing education than whether or not this was his ticket to stardom. "So she got on the phone and talked to Denise, AJ's mom, and Denise told her about the tutor, home schooling, how they go about their days getting their studies done. And if everything worked out, then I would just fall right in with AJ and Nick and be tutored together with them. That was her main concern, and it was all worked out. To make a long story short, we talked to management that night and they said, 'You gotta get down here and audition. We've heard a lot of great things about you and you gotta give it a shot.'"

"A lot of people think the entertainment business is such an enjoyable thing and glamorous. It has its perks, but, you know, there's real life behind all that."
— Brian talking about his 1998 heart surgery.

He was on a plane at 6 a.m. the next morning and flew to Orlando, where Kevin greeted him with a limo – which surely should have indicated that he was about to embark on something very different from what he was used to.

"I was scared half to death," Brian admitted. "Here I was and hours before I was talking to him on the phone. Now I'm down in Orlando, I'm in a limo . . . I was like, 'Wooahh, what have I gotten myself into? Here I am, from Lexington, a middle-class guy who is growing up and worked hard and, pow, overnight my life has changed.' Right when I met management I was like, 'This is for me, I can fit into this, I love this.' It was nothing like I expected. I expected it to be all formal, 'cause I had never auditioned for anything. I didn't know what it was going to be like."

Brian reaches out for a hug – from you!

Larry Busacca / Retna

Back In The Hospital

As pop history has revealed, the Backstreet Boys, after several years of struggling, would be destined to become one of the most successful current bands. But for Brian, often considered the soul of the band and the first member to compose a song for them, it hasn't always been easy. While touring with the Backstreet Boys in early 1998, he found himself unusually tired – more so than the grind of performing show after show would normally make him – and eventually checked himself into the hospital. Exams revealed that the hole in his heart, which had been there since childhood, was finally taking its toll. On May 8, 1998, an operation to repair the heart was performed and was a complete success. Two months to the day, he was back on stage with the Backstreet Boys, feeling better than he ever had before. The operation also gave him pause to reflect on all of the wonderful aspects of his life.

Brian during a rare quiet moment in 2000.

Mark Shenley / CP / Retna

"My initial thought when I heard the news was, 'Great timing,'" he told *Teen People.* "Quit Playin' Games (With My Heart)" was topping the charts and had opened the door for the Boys in the United States – finally – after they had made it big in Europe. The necessary operation would put him out of circulation for about two months. Rumors made the rounds that manager Louis Pearlman insisted that Brian put off the surgery for about six months so that the tour could be concluded. Throughout that time, Brian performed with an oxygen tank nearby in case he found it difficult to breathe. In an interview with MTV's John Norris, it was obvious that Brian resented what he was asked to do.

"It should have been nothing but my choice," he said, "but it was scheduled and you deal with it. A lot of stuff went down with that. A lot of trying times happened with our previous management. The schedule was just laid out in front of us, and that was what got so frustrating, because it was just chop, chop, chop. I had to be everywhere at a specific time, and nothing could stand in the way. After experiencing a delay in my surgery twice, then finally having it, eight weeks to the day of my surgery I was back up on stage in Charlotte, North Carolina."

Moving Toward The Future

It was, he admits, a scary period, as the situation put a lot of weight on the band's shoulders with each member having to decide what was more important: his health or carrying on with the tour. Although every Backstreet Boy agrees now that it was a mistake, at the time they decided they should go forward with the tour. "Everything happens for a reason," said Brian, "and it turned out good. Thank God that everything

Bernhard Kuhmstedt / Retna

The band (Brian is on the left) poses for a photo in Germany.

went well; that we didn't have to take too much time. I know there are a lot of loving and caring fans out there, and I got letters beyond belief of gratitude and thankfulness. But I think it shows them a different phase of what our work is like, because they realize a little bit through me, I think, how hard work is. A lot of people think the entertainment business is such an enjoyable thing and glamorous. It has its perks, but, you know, there's real life behind all that.

"The older I got, the more I realized that maybe God kept me on this earth so I could use the gift that he gave me to be a singer, to be an entertainer," he added. "Today, I have no physical limitations; it's all in the past. I look back on the experiences and I've learned from the past and I've put it into everyday life. It's just an experience that you can't get rid of, that you have to turn around and use to your benefit.

Dave Hogan / ImageDirect

Brian and his wife, Leighanne, make an appearance at the 2000 Grammy Awards in Los Angeles.

"I love being in the Backstreet Boys," he proclaimed. "I wouldn't change a thing in my life. It's a blessing. I thank God for everything. I think this group has a lot of potential. I think this group has longevity. We're for real – what you see is what you get. We're five solo artists put together and we love to do what we do."

To show his appreciation, Brian has made a point of using his celebrity to help charitable causes. What makes his efforts different from the charitable efforts of his fellow Backstreet Boys is that Brian is the only one with a foundation named after him. The Brian Littrell Endowment Fund and Brian

Frank Micelotta / ImageDirect

The band performs with Sting at the VH1 Men Strike Back concert in April of 2000. Brian is dressed in white.

Littrell's Healthy Heart Club both serve to help children with heart conditions, a cause that is near and dear to him.

Just as near and dear to him is actress Leighanne Wallace, who became his wife during the summer of 2000, thus making Brian the second member of the Backstreet Boys to take a wife. And just to show how sensitive a fiancé he was, the happy couple related to *J-14* magazine that the wedding plans were being made together. "It's a team effort and it always has to be when a relationship is involved," the too-good-to-be-true Brian told the magazine. "She's dreamed all of her life of having a fairy-tale wedding, and I'm going to do everything I possibly can to make her dreams come true." ♪

Brian Hits The Big Screen

Brian had a small role (he played the horse-drawn carriage driver) in the 2000 film *Olive Juice*. ♪

HOWIE D.

Kelly Swift / Retna

HOWIE D.

Birth Name
Howard Dwaine Dorough

Birth Date
August 22, 1973

Zodiac Sign
Leo

Birthplace
Orlando, Florida

Marital Status
Single

Favorites
Tom Hanks, R&B music

James Smeal / Ron Galella LTD

The Howie Dorough-ic age began on August 22, 1973 in Orlando, Florida, when he was born at Orange Memorial Hospital to his parents, Hoke, a police officer, and Paula, a housewife. Upon arriving at home – the house, incidentally, that he lived in his entire life before becoming a hit with the Backstreet Boys – Howie D. found a slightly crowded living arrangement, with four siblings (Angela, Caroline, Polly Anna and Johnny) waiting for him.

"My parents have been together for well over 40 years," he related in an autobiography written for the press. "There's 10 years' difference between me and the next youngest sibling, so I kind of came to my parents a little later in life."

But Howie didn't have to wait very long to discover his love for the spotlight. "When I was about three or four," he said, "I used to get up on my grandma's bed and sit with my little guitar and sing 'Baby Face'."

Following The Yellow Brick Road

He put this "career" on hold for a couple of years, until his sister Polly Anna was a senior in high school. She decided to get involved in the arts, and her first play was a stage version of *The Wizard of Oz*. She brought Howie along, and he scored a role as a member of the Lollipop Guild, while she portrayed Glenda the Good Witch.

"I remember having these pants that were like two sizes too big and I'd be dancing around holding my pants up," Howie said, looking back on the experience, "because they'd be falling down the whole time."

While the Wizard may have been doling out brains, hearts, courage and a home to other characters in the cast, this particular munchkin was given insight as to how he could draw maximum attention to himself on the stage.

Paul Smith / Retna

Howie smiles for the camera.

"I used to always pretend that I had stage fright," he sheepishly explained. "I'd go off to the side and I would put on this big act because I'd get so much attention. But as I got older, I really did start to get nervous before a show. I don't think nerves ever leave you. That's what keeps you going, those little butterflies. The day I lose that will be the day I lose touch with reality."

Girls? Or Career?

Throughout elementary school, he continued taking acting and voice lessons, and got himself involved with as many musicals as he could. This process continued into junior high, where, while his classmates were focusing on the opposite sex, he found that he couldn't really get involved in a relationship for fear that it would distract him from his career goals. His concern was that if he got involved with a girl – at least seriously involved – he would be spending all of his time thinking about her and not on the future and the career he decided that he wanted more than anything. “A lot of times,” Howie explained, “I’d end up having a girlfriend for two to three weeks, if I was lucky.”

> "There will never be an end to the Backstreet Boys. We'll constantly be doing reunion tours. But just like Boyz II Men, we'd like to do our own little projects, too."
>
> — Howie on the future of the band. ♪

During junior high and high school, Howie managed to hone his trademark falsetto style. “I would sing higher notes than the girls next to me,” he said. “I sang in the children’s choir at my church, and then I went into the men’s choir. I sang throughout high school.” Indeed, in high school he saw the impact his singing could have on an audience when he entered a talent show. “When I sang ‘Unchained Melody,’ I hit the high note and got a standing ovation,” he told *Teen People* magazine. “When I was done, they didn’t even want to [see] any more people. They were ready to give me the award.”

He also gave acting a shot, inspired by Polly Anna, who has gone on to be a singer and an actress. He served as an extra (in a classroom scene) in the Ron Howard film *Parenthood,* and had a small role in the Burt Reynolds movie *Cop And A Half.* Several commercials for Disney World followed, and then a starring role for a

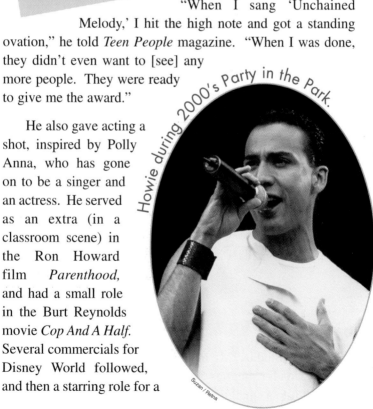

Howie during 2000's Party in the Park.

Suzan / Retna

Nickelodeon pilot called *Welcome Freshmen,* which, unfortunately did not go to series (although maybe in the long run it was actually a good thing). Howie admits, though, he would have been fine had his career taken him in a thespian direction.

Howie at the 2000 American Music Awards.

James Smeal / Ron Galella LTD

"Acting and singing are like one for me," said Howie, whose musical tastes include Jon Secada and Earth Wind & Fire's Philip Bailey. "I was either going out for an acting audition or I was in a talent competition. I tried to keep them both equal so whichever one took off first was the one I was going to go with."

The Backstreet Boys Come Together

It was during this process of attempting to see which faction of his career would take off that Howie met AJ McLean. They had the same vocal coach, who introduced the two young men. The two of them became fast friends and they soon came into contact with 13-year-old Nick Carter, whose talent was electric.

Howie's Hobbies

In his spare time, Howie says he likes to water ski, lift weights, swim and play a little racquetball. ♪

"We kept running into each other all the time at auditions," Howie noted to the press. "We all did stuff for Nickelodeon, Disney, MGM Studios. We met through acting and found out we had a passion for singing. So we put a little group together and then took it to a small record label in Orlando."

That joining of forces, of course, ultimately led to the formation of the Backstreet Boys and a true pop phenomenon that has captured the world and touched the hearts of millions of fans around the world. Fans, Howie emphasizes, who mean the world to the band.

"We do try to gain the love of our fans," he told *Big Bop* magazine. "Every place I go, at the end of every show, I always say, 'Hey, the Backstreet Boys will never break your heart.' We want them to know that we're not planning to just come and go like some other boyfriend may do – or some other group. We care about our fans. Meeting people, getting a chance to perform for them and seeing them enjoy your music is one of the better parts of the job. One of the most gratifying things is seeing people sing your songs out in the audience along with you.

"I think we all hoped and dreamed about it," Howie said at a foreign press conference regarding their success. "You can never expect it. But I think it's a blessing. We thank God every day for helping us. We've gotten a chance to travel around the world, to see new places, see new cultures, try new foods. The worst thing is being away from our families."

Jim Smeal / Ron Galella LTD

Howie (center) and the rest of the band celebrate the success of their debut album at a Los Angeles event in 1998.

Fame Is Great, But Family Is #1

Which brings up an interesting point about the Backstreet Boys as a whole: despite all the trappings of success, they all seem extremely well-rooted, primarily because of the closeness between them and their families. It is, to say the least, unusual in the high-gloss pop world. The point is driven home by something Howie did when he and the band first started pulling in big bucks.

James Smeal / Ron Galella LTD

Howie at the 2000 Billboard Music Awards in Las Vegas.

"The first thing I did with my money was put central heating in my parents' house," he told *Big Bop* magazine. "It's about 100 years old and it has, like, the nice hardwood floors and stuff, but no central heating. So I put it in throughout the whole house.

"Now I'm fixing up their place by landscaping the backyard and the front yard. We've got a lot of plants in there now and I got my mom an elephant water fountain, because her biggest thing is elephants."

At a press conference he went on to admit, "I'm Mr. Souvenir man. My mom collects elephants, so normally wherever I go I get her an elephant. One of my older sisters wants postcards, so I send her a postcard from whatever country we visit. My little nieces like those little dolls dressed up. By the time I go home, I have to get an extra suitcase to carry everything. But it's cool.

"For me," he told *Teen Beat,* "my best memories were always Christmas times at home with all my family and my mom and dad and the young ones. I have five nieces and one nephew. I was an uncle at four years old."

Much of this feeling for family undoubtedly comes from the nurturing environment he grew up in, particularly from older siblings who were always looking out for him. "They would take me around to their high school and show me off to their friends," he wrote. "They didn't really tell me what to do but I would always go to them for advice on girls or school. I feel as if I was sheltered somewhat with my siblings giving me advice about all this stuff. I felt grown up mentally about a lot of the decisions I made, but then a lot of times it is hard for me to make those decisions because I hadn't had a lot of opportunity to make them. Of course, I'm older now and more experienced."

His Dream Date

Howie has said that his dream date would be a candlelight dinner, followed by a movie or dancing and then ending with a long walk on the beach. ♪

What's Next?

The biggest question for Howie, personally, is what the future will hold. Apparently, he's being really smart with his

Howie looks "larger than life" on stage at a recent concert.

Simon Ritter / Retna

money, investing it in a company he's started called Sweet D., Inc., which develops condominiums on Florida's east coast, and using family members to run it. Then there is always the possibility of a film career, as acting is something he has started to yearn to follow again. "For me," he told *16,* "it's like I'm always acting – acting and singing is like one for me. It's all one – it's all entertainment. My favorite actor is Tom Hanks because I really like the way he switches from drama to comedy, and that's what I'd like to be able to do."

Howie rehearses before the 2000 Grammy Awards.

Dave Hogan / ImageDirect

Then there's the issue of the Backstreet Boys themselves. Every time the group reaches another plateau, many doomsayers in the press insist that their time as a band is limited. The media tries to predict that the success the band has worked so hard for will ultimately splinter them apart from each other. Howie doesn't see this as a possibility, though he did once get a taste of what being on his own would be like when he went by himself on a South American promotional tour several years ago.

"Success is all great, but at the end of the day . . . it just makes you realize that nothing is more important than your own life or the life of a family member of yours."

— Howie on the death of his sister, Caroline.

"It was a great experience, but weird without the others around," Howie told the British press. "That's when it really hit me, the loneliness of not having the four guys around me. You appreciate the things you take for granted, like having a big group to be with. It is good to have the five of us bonding with each other. We usually don't have our families with us, so that is why it is good to have brothers like these guys and to be so close."

As to a potential break-up, he told *Live & Kicking* magazine, "There will never be an end to the Backstreet Boys. We'll constantly be doing reunion tours. But just like Boyz II Men, we'd like to do our own little projects, too. It's something we're very open-minded about for the future."

Howie D.'s Loss

While life as a Backstreet Boy is all well and good, absolutely nothing has touched Howie in the way that the death of his sister Caroline – from lupus, in September 1998 – has. To help cope with this loss, he created the Caroline Dorough Cochran Lupus Memorial Foundation at Florida Hospital, and addressed the pain in the band's video for "Show Me The Meaning Of Being Lonely."

AP/WWP

The band (Howie is on the left) accepts a World Music Award in 1998.

"With my sister passing away," he confessed to MTV, "that was the very closest thing for me, the feeling of being lonely, and knowing that I no longer had that one fifth of my family there, and knowing how it felt when she passed away. I literally had to get on a plane right after her funeral that day, to go to South America to perform a concert the next day. It was one of the first couple of concerts that we ever canceled in the history of the Backstreet Boys. We knew when we got started in the whole thing that there would be a lot of things we would have to sacrifice. I figured the guys would probably go on, but it was something that was a big enough impact on everybody that they decided, 'Let's just take this time off here and reschedule it.'"

Howie added that the tragedy was something he would never wish on anyone, and not something you could even contemplate in your day-to-day living. "This success is all great," he explained, "but at the end of the day, with certain situations, like Brian's heart surgery or with a family member passing away, it just makes you realize that nothing is more important than your own life or the life of a family member of yours."

Kevin Winter / ABC / ImageDirect

The guys grin as they show off their 2000 Radio Music Award, which Howie is holding.

Interestingly, the "Show Me The Meaning Of Being Lonely" video has played a large part in Howie's mom being able to deal with the pain. "It touched my mom a lot," he told

Howie Hits The Clubs

Howie owns a club in Orlando called Tabu, where he has been known to get on stage and perform hip-hop routines. ♪

the press. "At the time we had a lot of people coming to the house and giving sympathy cards and putting a lot of donations toward the foundation. Out of all of us, my mom took it the hardest. It's one thing having your parent pass away, but having your own daughter or your own son pass away . . . I think now, with the video and everything, she watches the video and I swear, I think it actually helps her move on. She's able to talk about it. She's able just to move on with life."

Such is often the power of music, and certainly the power of the Backstreet Boys: their music is something that can embrace you like a warm blanket, and help ease away some of the burdens of your life. It's that little bit of magic that each of us can use sometimes. ♪

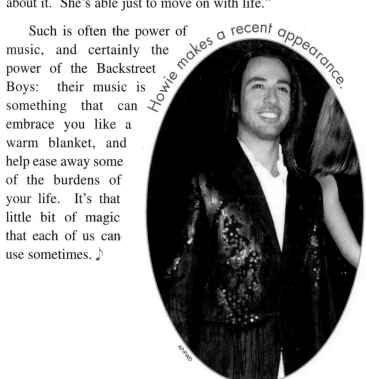

Howie makes a recent appearance.

AP/FWD

B. Khan / Retna

KEVIN

KEVIN

Birth Name
Kevin Scott Richardson

Birth Date
October 3, 1971

Zodiac Sign
Libra

Birthplace
Lexington, Kentucky

Marital Status
Married to Kristin Willits

Favorites
Elton John, Billy Joel

The other Backstreet Boys have described Kevin, the oldest member of the band, as a big brother. A more appropriate title might be field general.

Ever since the group's now-repaired rift with management, Kevin has acted as the group's leader, insisting that they couldn't let up just because they'd had some success. They had to keep improving. "My dad was probably the one that instilled that in me," Kevin revealed in a press conference. He would always tell Kevin that if he couldn't do a good job, then he shouldn't do the job at all.

Kevin took that advice to heart and as the Backstreet Boys continue to grow as a group, his work ethic certainly would make his late father proud.

Eyeing The Sky

Kevin was born on October 3, 1971, to Jerald and Ann Richardson, the family's third son after siblings Jerald Jr. and Tim. His early years were spent on a farm in Harrisburg, Kentucky, where he and his brothers spent their time hiking, riding dirt bikes and horses and working the farm. It was here, lying in a field behind the family house and looking up at the sky, that Kevin discovered his first passion – not music, but flying.

"I wanted to be up there in the clouds," he admitted in an interview. "I wanted to fly jet planes. I started thinking about joining the Air Force."

Wilberto Boogaard Sunshine / Retna

Kevin takes a moment out of his busy schedule to smile for the camera.

When he was 9, Kevin got a little bit closer to the clouds when the family moved to the Appalachian Mountain region of Kentucky and a town named Beattyville. There, his father was put in charge of a summer camp. During the winter, the family had the 17-room log cabin to themselves, while during the warmer weather, Kevin found himself making new friends every few weeks as a new batch of children attended the camp. He described it as living two separate lives. During the school year, he and his brothers would take the bus to school, where he had a variety of regular friends he would hang out with. During the summer, however, he wouldn't see those friends because he would be working at the camp with his father, whom he was close to.

"It was a church camp," he told *Tiger Beat*. "I was fortunate to grow up there. I had tons of friends because every summer the camp was full of kids my age. I met people from all over the state and sometimes from all over the country as well. There was no reason to leave at all – all these people to talk to, play with, to meet. There were lots of cute girls. I'd get my heart broken every summer, because I would find a girlfriend and then she would leave and I wouldn't see her again."

Kevin Finds A New Love

At about the same time he was involved at the summer camp, Kevin discovered his natural talent for singing and playing piano. "I taught myself to play by ear," he related at a press conference. "My grandfather, my grandmother and all their brothers and sisters learned to play piano by ear. My whole family sings. I grew up singing. Me and my mom, who is Brian's [Littrell's] father's sister, sang together in church."

Taking To The Sky

Kevin has taken flying lessons and was allowed to practice his skills on a recent flight to Tokyo. "The best moment of the whole 9 1/2 hour flight though was when I put my flying lessons to good use and took the controls. Man, what a feeling," he told Backstreet Boys fans about the experience. ♪

Almost immediately, Kevin fell in love with music – a passion he soon passed along to his cousin, Brian. "I used to sing into a hairbrush in front of my bedroom mirror," he said. "Brian and I used to harmonize all the time."

A young Kevin smiles shyly at the camera.

Mark Cairns / Retna

Kevin's love for music also came from a large number of bands he heard on the radio, among them Prince, the Eagles, Boyz II Men, Van Halen, Aerosmith, Elton John, Billy Joel and New Edition. "I have a real variety of musical tastes," he said. "I just love music."

Kevin's parents recognized the seriousness

with which Kevin approached his love of music, and when he was a freshman in high school, they gave him a keyboard as a present. Thrilled, he practiced continually, achieving a level of competence that allowed him to perform a solo music act at local weddings and restaurants.

Kevin at the 2000 Grammy Awards.

Dave Hogan / ImageDirect

Bitten by the stage bug, he also tried out for and was cast in local theatrical productions of Neil Simon's *Barefoot In The Park* and *Bye, Bye Birdie.* Passionate about all kinds of performing, he also took up dancing and he made extra cash as a professional ballroom dance instructor.

"I want to have a family someday. Family is very important to me."
— Kevin on what he would like to do in the future. ♪

As he made his way through high school, he began to question what he wanted to do with his life. He knew that he still wanted to join the Air Force, maybe even apply to the Air Force Academy after graduation. There was also a love for playing sports. In fact, Hoover Niece, the football coach at Kevin's high school, Estill County High, reflected to the *Lexington Herald-Leader,* "He was Dr. Jekyll and Mr. Hyde on and off the football field. He played a hard-hitting game, while he was very much, 'Yes, sir; no, sir,' off the field."

In the same article Kevin added with a laugh, "I loved contact. I loved hitting people. I think it was a release for me. Now that I look back, I wish I would've played a more mental game because sometimes I was over-aggressive and I would overrun a play. I would've been a better player if I could've just controlled it a little more. But I was just out of control."

Some of that aggression, he's admitted, is still there. "I dance real aggressive, real hard," he said. "There are songs that are hard dance routines where you dance hard and real physical, and there are routines where you dance smooth, where you're like a cool cat; a Fred Astaire–type vibe."

Despite his fascination with the sky and love of sports, in the end Kevin decided that he didn't want to give up performing. His love of music prevailed.

Henry Lamb / Ron Galella LTD

Kevin (left) and Nick answer questions at a 1999 press conference at New York City's Studio 54.

Deciding that Kentucky would ultimately prove stifling to his blossoming abilities, Kevin moved to Orlando, Florida, after high school to break into the entertainment field. When he wasn't at auditions, he paid the bills working as a guide at Disney World. This, in turn, led to him scoring the role of Aladdin and a Ninja Turtle in two of Disney World's stage shows. While some might laugh at the idea of Kevin hanging out with Mickey and the gang, he found it to be a positive experience. "It helped turn me more into a people person," he admitted to the press. "You have to be outgoing to be a guide. Before that I was a much more quiet person."

Tragedy Strikes

As Kevin's responsibilities at the theme park increased, his parents decided to come down to Florida to see how their youngest son was doing. The reunion was "wonderful," but it was capped with tragic news: Kevin's father had been diagnosed with colon cancer. "It had already spread through his body when I was told," Kevin has said. "I was devastated. I moved back home to Kentucky to be with him. He lived for 10 months after his diagnosis."

Bill Davila / Retna

Kevin is caught on camera as he strolls through New York's Greenwich Village.

His father died in 1991. "I was very angry," Kevin admitted in an interview. "I felt my father had been cheated of his golden years. He was only 49. But eventually I realized my family is not unique. You have to go on."

He has gone on, but it hasn't always been easy without his father there to guide him. "I miss his advice," Kevin said. "I talked to him about what I wanted to do with my life. I was going to join the Air Force when I left high school. That was the logical thing, my brain told me to do that, whereas my heart told me to pursue my music. It was my dad who told me to go with my heart."

Picking Up The Pieces

Still mourning, Kevin went back to Florida after his father's funeral and resumed work at Disney World. As he gained confidence as a performer, he began to land solo singing gigs outside the theme park and eventually he heard about a fledgling group that was seeking members. "There were two other members who didn't work out," he reflected to the press, "and I replaced one of them. Then we needed another member and I called Brian."

The guys pose together for a group shot.

B. Khan / Retna

Brian was the last piece of the puzzle, and the Backstreet Boys were born. One important aspect of the group's success is that it has allowed Kevin to deal with the pain of losing his father by participating in charity drives and visiting sick children. And those activities have given him a unique perspective on the pop star's life.

"I want to live my life in a way that would make my father proud. As long as I do what makes me happy, without sacrificing my morals, he'll be proud."

— Kevin on his relationship with his father, who died in 1991.

"I don't want to be out on the road all my life," he told *Tiger Beat.* "I want to have a family someday. Family is very important to me. But I don't think I could manage a family and be the kind of father I need to be when traveling out on the road all the time."

After all, his own father is still a major influence on his life – especially when he's on tour with the group. The world is handed to pop stars on a silver platter, and many celebrities can lose themselves in alcohol, drugs and arrogant, mean-spirited behavior toward women. But Kevin – setting an example that the other Backstreet Boys follow – doesn't let himself go down fame's dark road.

Kevin signs CDs at a Virgin megastore.

Suzan / Retna

"I want to live my life in a way that would make my father proud," he said. "As long as I do what makes me happy, without sacrificing my morals, he'll be proud."

Sexiest Pop Star Alive!

As the popularity of the Backstreet Boys continued to grow, it became pretty obvious that the press and the fans couldn't get enough of the band, either as a group or as individuals. This was driven home to Kevin when he returned to the Lexington, Kentucky, area to perform a concert. Local news coverage was amazing and the populace was thrilled. "I'm so thrilled to be playing here," Kevin told the *Citizen Voice And Times*. "It means a lot to me to be able to play in front of my family and friends, and I'm glad after all the touring that we were able to play here in Rupp Arena. It's cool, because we're more in the central part of Kentucky, so everybody can have a chance to come."

> Did You Know . . .
>
> . . . that when Kevin is out on the road, he takes an envelope filled with pictures of his family with him? ♪

He admitted that things changed a bit in terms of the press after the Backstreet Boys' second American album, *Millennium*, sold seven million copies. Suddenly the press scrutiny grew more intense with all sorts of rumors flying around. Whereas coverage had previously been pretty positive, suddenly the band was being nit-picked to death.

"Something I came to realize in the past year," Kevin said during an on-line chat, "which initially bothered me, but now I've accepted, is the fact that you just can't please everybody. Everybody is not gonna like our music. Everyone is not gonna like us. The main thing for us is we just want people to know that everything they hear on the album is real. It's us. It's our voices singing. It's us coming up with the treatments for our videos and the ideas for our tours, the stage show, pulling it together. We're just not guys who are told what to do or where to be."

Larry Busacca / Retna

Kevin looking cool in blue shades and a denim jacket.

Kevin has proven that point again and again in a number of different ways. First was when *PEOPLE* magazine proclaiming him the sexiest pop star alive in their 1999 poll. "It's time to separate the man from the boys," wrote the magazine. "With his laser-bright green eyes and chiseled chin, Richardson was deemed the group's 'Most Likely Future Male Model' by *The New York Times.*"

"That was fun," Kevin told the *Citizen Voice And Times.* "It was nice, but I remember back in high school some of the fellas used to joke with me and called me pretty boy, and I'm just thinking, 'Oh, great!'"

A Dream Comes True – Times Two!

Then, he finally lived his lifelong dream of taking to the sky when the Air Force jet performers the Blue Angels invited a Backstreet Boy on board for one of their flights. "The guys know about my flying dreams," Kevin told *Teen People.* "Eventually I'm going to get my private license. So they said, 'You go ahead.' Everybody asked, 'Is it dangerous?' I was like, 'They're trained military pilots. I'm in the safest hands possible.'" After the flight he summed up the experience as follows: "It's the difference between riding in a station wagon and riding in a Lamborghini."

Most exciting, of course, was Kevin's recent marriage to longtime girlfriend, actress/dancer Kristin Willits. "We've been through a lot together," he related to MTV, "but she knew me when I was a Ninja Turtle. I met her in the cafeteria at Walt Disney World. She walked into the cafeteria, and it was like someone turned a light on. We were both working there. She was a dancer. She's been on Broadway, done lots of things. Being in the business, she definitely has an appreciation for it. You need somebody that can understand a lot."

Jim Smeal / Ron Galella LTD

Kevin and wife Kristin at the 2000 Vanity Fair Magazine Oscar Party in Hollywood.

Understanding probably will be necessary, because it hasn't exactly been easy for Mr. and Mrs. Richardson to settle down into a regular married life. At the time they got married, Kevin was involved with a Backstreet Boys tour while simultaneously recording the group's *Black And Blue* CD, and Willits' career was heating up, with a co-starring role in the Jennifer Aniston/Mark Wahlberg feature film, *Metal God.*

Nonetheless, despite the difficulties of careers that travel in different directions, everyone is convinced they're going to make it.

Opined Kevin's brother Tim to the *Lexington Herald-Leader,* "They're two good people. Remove all the glamour and the fact that he's a Backstreet Boy, that they're in the entertainment industry, and they're just two people who love each other. You want them to have a solid, committed marriage. That's the most important thing to them right now. Because when all the fame is gone, they will have each other."

Doing His Part

Kevin devotes a great deal of his spare time to Just Within Reach, the environmental foundation he started in late 2000. ♪

Family remains the most important thing to Kevin, whether it's the bond that has been formed between him and the other members of the Backstreet Boys, or the ones he has with his family and wife. Some things will never change. ♪

Frank Micelotta / ABC / ImageDirect

Kevin shakes hands with singer Wayne Newton while the rest of the band looks on at the 2000 Radio Music Awards.

John Gladwin / Retna

NICK

NICK

Birth Name:
Nicholas Gene Carter

Birth Date:
January 20, 1980

Zodiac Sign
Aquarius

Birthplace:
Jamestown, New York

Marital Status
Single

Favorites
Cheese pizza, Twix, video games

Nick Carter, the youngest member of the Backstreet Boys, gave every indication that he was destined for a successful career in the entertainment world even before he could talk!

Born on January 20, 1980, in Jamestown, New York, to Bob and Jane Carter, young Nick spent his earliest years helping his parents and grandmother run a popular dance club known as the Yankee Rebel, which is where he first demonstrated his moves to an audience.

"We had a little dance floor at the Yankee Rebel," Nick related to the press, "and my dad was a DJ and played records. When I was real small, I used to get up there in my diapers and dance around."

He loved the attention, but he never got a chance to follow up on his dream of seriously performing at the club. When Nick was 6 and his younger sister, Bobbie Jean (B.J.), was 2, their parents decided to head south. "They thought maybe it'd be cool to move down to Florida and start a different business," Nick said in a self-penned bio for the press. "So they packed up their old Cadillac El Dorado, loaded all our stuff into a little trailer and we took off."

The Carter family's first home in the Sunshine State was in a quiet retirement community, for which Nick's parents worked. There, he and B.J. made their own fun – or at least Nick remembers it as being fun. "Me and B.J. used to get into so much mischief, it was so funny," Nick fondly recalls. "One of my favorite things to do in the backyard was to go swinging on the hammock we had. I'd have B.J. on it, and I'd twist her up in it, let go and watch her spin. She kept spinning until she'd get all dizzy, and then she'd go tell Mom. This was a big backyard and the senior citizens really didn't care what we did."

Mark Shenley / CP / Retna

Nick flashes his pearly whites for the camera.

The Carter family continued to grow, providing Nick with even more victims for his mischief. First came another sister, Leslie, and then twins – a sister and brother named Angel and Aaron. In Nick's opinion, the addition of his younger siblings made life better for him. "I guess you could say it was a happy change, because now I have lots of siblings," he said. "My dad, who's an only child, got all the attention from his parents when he was a kid, but he had to make friends. I could make friends, but I always knew I had someone to play with and hang out with."

Nick And The Phantom

While attending elementary school, Nick took his first stab at acting, starring in a school production of *The Phantom Of The Opera.* Nick wasn't the director's first choice for the role of the Phantom, but when the student who was originally picked discovered that he couldn't quite sing the necessary high notes, Nick was asked to take over. By the time opening night rolled around, the director and many others were convinced that Nick had a special talent. Nick's mom, Jane, was one of the believers, and she agreed to allow Nick to develop his talent. Which he did. In fact, there's even a rumor that he was in Tim Burton's movie *Edward Scissorhands.*

"I'm a very quiet person. I consider myself a modern-day hermit. I don't like to party. I'm happy if I'm in my hotel room just chillin'."

— Nick on what he's like off stage.

"It would be going too far to say I was actually in *Edward Scissorhands,*" he related at a press conference, "because I was so far in the background that you can't tell it's me. It would be better to say I was on the set of the film . . . I was in the scene when Edward looks out of a window to the neighborhood. For a split second, he sees some kids playing – one of them was me. I was sliding on a yellow piece of plastic we used to call a Slip n' Slide. They were long, flat sheets with water coming out of holes and were really popular with kids at the time. I had to slide on one in the background of a

Nick doing what he does best – performing!

Melanie Edwards / Retna

shot. It was great fun being on the set, but it was really cold and they made us do it a lot of times."

Mickey Or The Boys?

Nick hams it up in a Sears commercial.

Bill Davila / Retna

When the family moved again the following year to the Orlando, Florida, area, an entertainment boom town thanks to the presence of Disney World and Universal Studios, Nick found himself in a new elementary school. But he never really got to feel at home at this school. He'd begun to seriously pursue his dream of being a performer, which often kept him out of class (he worked with tutors to keep up with his studies). "I did plays and commercials and sang in a few places," he said. "I did commercials for the lottery and the Money Store. I'd really decided that I wanted to be a performer, so I auditioned for the *Mickey Mouse Club* show and the Backstreet Boys."

"Being on my own, with just the silence of the sea, is such an escape from the constant pressure of being on tour. It's something I need to do – just to get away from it all."

— Nick loves to be out on his sailboat. ♪

And he got both gigs, which left Nick with a huge decision: dancing and singing with Mickey, or hitting the road with the Boys. Naturally, he chose Mickey Mouse.

Then he changed his mind. It was a tougher call than one might think now. After all, the *Mickey Mouse Club* was known for launching careers of teen stars (Britney Spears, Christina Aguilera, JC Chasez, Justin Timberlake and Keri Russell, for example). As for the Backstreet Boys . . . well, the group didn't even have a record deal! The act had started coming together when AJ, Howie and Nick answered an ad placed in the *Orlando Sentinel* by Louis Pearlman. The trio tried harmonizing and found that they sounded great together. They obtained a manager (Johnny Wright) as a result, and would eventually be joined by Kevin and Brian.

Growing Up Fast

But despite the group's uncertain prospects, 13-year-old Nick could recognize talent, and he saw it in the others. Ultimately, and with his parents' support, he decided to be a Backstreet Boy.

"It was kind of scary," he admitted. "There were meetings and talk about what it would take for the Backstreet Boys to get a record produced. We sang at malls and in local places. On the road, I turned out to be the one who liked to sleep the most. AJ ate the most – and I pulled the most practical jokes."

Karen Hoyt / ImageDirect

Nick rehearses for an upcoming concert. Howie can be seen in the background.

Later, in the pages of *Teen* magazine, Nick reflected on the group's early years. "When we first started," he explained, "there was a big difference between me and the next youngest, AJ, who was 16. But I've learned a lot over the years in terms of how to communicate, how to be respectful and how not to be a pest, which I was when I was younger. I like to get a laugh out of things. I was a prankster back then. Now I'm a very quiet person. I consider myself a modern-day hermit. I don't like to party. I'm happy if I'm in my hotel room just chillin'."

But those first couple of years weren't all fun and games for the young singing group. Their inexperience was a hindrance. "A big lesson that we've learned," Nick told the press, "is that it's not as easy as it looks. We first thought that you sign a contract, you get to go into the studio and you're handed a big check. It's not really like that. It's a lot of hard work. In the end, hopefully, things will pay off. But, I mean, it's really not as easy as it seems."

Henry Lamb / Ron Galella LTD

Nick takes a break at the 1999 Houston Street Court Special Concert for Disney benefit.

It was indeed a lot of work, and after two years and very little success, there were times when the Boys questioned whether they were ever going to get their big break. But their chance did finally come when their second single went gold in Germany. After a sell-out tour overseas, they returned home where the U.S. public was finally ready for their special brand of music.

But there have been prices to pay. For one thing, Nick acknowledges that he lost out on a lot by not going to school, playing sports or going to his high school prom. "I think it was a definite sacrifice to make in order to do this," he told Yahoo about choosing show business over childhood. "But at the same time, I wouldn't give this up for the world, although, as I've said, there are things I wish I could have done."

During those early days – and on those rare occasions – when Nick wasn't touring or in the studio, he lived with the rest of his family in Tampa Bay, Florida, and escaped from it all on a boat he bought for himself.

"To be honest, I've never really fallen in love. The day I find the girl of my dreams, I will spoil her rotten. I'll just be about us. Faithfulness is very important to me."

— Nick reflects on the girl of his dreams.

"I fill the engine with petrol and just head out to sea," he told the foreign press. "The Florida Keys are the greatest stretch of ocean in the world, with lots of small islands you can stop off at. Many a time I've played football on the beach with my brothers and sisters. A lot of the time I go out on the boat alone. Being on my own, with just the silence of the sea, is such an escape from the constant pressure of being on tour. It's something I need to do – just to get away from it all. To me, the Florida Keys is paradise on earth."

Chris Pizzello / ABC / ImageDirect

Nick (center) and the band show off their 2000 Radio Music Award.

Does Nick bring girls out on his boat? Absolutely, he revealed. "We swim in the sea and play around, but I never try to kiss them," he said. "That's the way I prefer it [right now]. I don't really want to fall in love yet. I prefer to wait a little bit. To be honest, I've never really fallen in love. I've just never felt this strong sensation. Of course, in the past there have been girls who were important to me. I went out with this girl called Bryn for about a year. The day I find the girl of my dreams, I will spoil her rotten. It'll just be about us. Faithfulness is very important to me. I couldn't go out with a girl who liked other guys. And I would be incapable of cheating on my girlfriend. I wouldn't be able to look her straight in the eye. When I have a girlfriend, I won't even need to look at other girls."

Nick relaxes during Super Bowl rehearsals.

Rick Diamond / ImageDirect

The impression Nick gives is of a sweet guy who's had his heart broken in the past. "Not exactly," he said in an on-line interview. The problem was that before he became a Backstreet Boy, he never had the chance to have his heart broken. "When I was at school," he said, "I used to look at all the pretty girls and wish they'd go out with me, but they were only interested in the cool guys who were really into sports. I wasn't very popular in school. The girls just didn't want to know me. I was really small and no one paid me much attention. That's what makes being

What Nick Listens To

Nick cites Steve Perry (of Journey), Boyz II Men, Michael Jackson, Nirvana and Jodeci among his musical influences. ♪

called a 'babe' nowadays so weird. I'm really honored that people see me in that light, but I don't really understand it. Now the first thing I look for is a girl with a good heart. Looks definitely come in second. It taught me not to judge people by the way they look -- it's what's inside that counts."

He remembers that when he was younger, he definitely suffered from a serious case of shyness. "When I was in school," he told *Teen People* magazine, "I wasn't very attractive to girls. But I remember a girl who I dated who was sweet and really kind. I've dated girls who might not have been that attractive, but they were just as kind and as sweet-hearted as anybody."

While love isn't at the top of his must-accomplish list right now, this thoughtful Backstreet Boy does have things he wants to accomplish outside of the group. One of them is to use his singing stardom to make the jump to the big screen.

Steve Granitz / Retna

Nick and his brother, singing sensation Aaron Carter, (shown here at the 2000 Billboard Music Awards) prove that good looks run in the family!

"I want to be a movie actor," he told the press. "I would love to do an action movie. It's got to be action. I would also like to direct a movie."

Dispelling The Rumors

Nick has admitted that success has often brought with it stress and tensions, most notably a bit of a falling out with his mother, reportedly over a relationship he was involved in; and then the problems of the media reporting – or making up! – stories on virtually every part of his life.

AP / WWP

Nick reaches out to the audience during a concert.

Regarding his mother and the supposed relationship issue, he told an MTV interviewer, "It was deeper than that. I think that was a scapegoat for a lot of other things that were going on. Really, everything right now is extremely cool. I love my family. Right now, I wanna be with my family and not talk business. That is probably the big issue. Now it's more just about me wanting to have my family out of the business, 'cause I deal with it so much, I'm living the business. So I wanna just take a break and get away from it. So that's pretty much what it's all about. I'm in the spotlight all the time, and everybody's in the spotlight, so a lot of people know your business."

As to the press and the rumors that are reported as facts, he told a Yahoo online chat crowd, "The rumors were that I was gay. I'm not gay. Also, that I was leaving the group. I'm not. I heard another one that I was kicked off the tour on the way to the show – I don't know how that could happen. That's a

Watch Out For Nick!

Nick is known as the prankster among the guys in the band. One of his most famous practical jokes was to give his friends fish-flavored gum. Yuck! ♪

couple of them. One reporter said I called Asian fans 'rude' and 'stupid'. I did not say that. That was a set-up by someone. I was framed and I'm very, very angry about it. I'd never say something like that, because our Malaysian fans are cool and loyal – they've been the best."

Nick does his best to put these aggravating stories behind him, focusing, instead, on what he and the other members of the Backstreet Boys are trying to do for their fans.

"I think Backstreet Boys music is made up of different types of music," he said on-line. "It's a mixture of R&B, pop and dance music. There are a lot of people out there who like variety. What we have to do is keep re-creating while the people are growing with you. You have to make sure that it's something new and something that's catchy to their ears, and it's something that they're going to enjoy listening to. Our job as entertainers and as recording artists is to make music for everyone out there that they will enjoy." ♪

The Backstreet Boys win yet another award!

Ethan Miller / Corbis

Q & A – What The Backstreet Boys Are All About

After returning from an exhausting four-day, six-continent world tour to thank their fans in late 2000, AJ, Brian, Howie, Kevin and Nick sat down to answer some questions about the tour, their *Black & Blue* album and how well they REALLY get along. Here's what they had to say!

Q: What can we expect from your tour [the first leg of which kicked off in January 2000] this time around?

AJ McLean: This has got to be the most incredible sensation we could feel, to come back to the U.S., after being around the world – we covered the entire Earth in four days! But there's only one person who did this, besides us . . . and that was [astronaut] John Glenn! Thank you so much for being here! We have the Black & Blue Army — there was the KISS army, and now we have the Black & Blue Army!

Howie Dorough: We're going to do, all the way up to March, touring all over America, mostly arenas during the first leg, and when we come, for the second leg, it's going to be stadiums, in the summertime. We'll be playing lots of stuff from [*Black & Blue*], and also material from the last couple of albums.

AP/WWP

Two young Backstreet Boys fans wait outside a hotel in Rio de Janeiro, Brazil, hoping to spot members of the band.

Q: Welcome back to New York City. Talk to me about happened in Rio, especially being on the bus.

Nick Carter: That was amazing. What happened is, we came into the airport, and we drove off in a little bus to do some interviews, and on the way to the hotel, we started to see that there were a lot of fans, a lot of people there, and then they started crowding the bus, and we went to a hotel, and the next day, it turned out that there were 40,000 people in front of the hotel, and it was an amazing feeling, all the energy. It didn't seem real.

Q: The Beatles came out with a greatest hits album – how do you compare yourselves to them?

Kevin Richardson: I don't think we feel worthy of comparisons to the Beatles — the hysteria that surrounds us, there are some similarities there, because they had quite a following and quite a young following, but to be compared musically to legends like the Beatles – it's a nice compliment.

Q: Are there any singles in the near future that you'll sing in Spanish?

AJ: Hopefully we'll be doing some translations for this new album.

Kevin: Off the first album, we recorded two songs in Spanish . . . so hopefully we'll be doing songs from this album as well.

Howie: From *Millennium*, we had a song dedicated to all our Spanish fans, called "Spanish Eyes." And that track had a little Latin flavor to it. I'm Puerto Rican, so . . . my amigos here are learning Latin.

Q: You guys are superheroes in a comic book right now . . . tell us about that?

Nick: Well, the idea was mine . . . I've always wanted to be a comic book character! What happened was, about 5 or 6 years ago, while we were touring in Europe, I brought an idea to the fellows. I was sketching out stuff and making up ideas about making up a comic. And they were like, "whatever, kid." So I decided to get a powerhouse team, Stan Lee Media, you know Stan Lee – he did Spider Man, and he's pretty much the bomb, and he put together the Backstreet Project for us. And it's an awesome series – every month there's a webisode and you can watch it. It's just a dream come true, you know – it's something I've always wanted to do, and thank God, being in a group like this, I can complete my dream.

Q: Is it true you have an on-line "Street Team" of fans?

Kevin: I think to have the fans working for you – they're more passionate than anybody. We thought it was a great idea, along with our management. Not only do we have the media, but we also have a Street Team of fans helping us promote the record. That's powerful – that's something you can do differently, rather than just using the television and media outlets. So that was a great idea, and we were happy to be able to make it happen, and we want to thank our Street Team.

Brazilian fans scream with joy as BSB arrives.

Reuters/Paulo Whitaker/Corbis

Brian Littrell: It was funny, when we decided to make the album cover half black and half blue – it was Nick's idea – he said we should get these little black and blue flags and have our black and blue army all over the world. So we thought it was a very cool concept, the way it all fit together in the end, and we're hoping to have those little black and blue flags flying high during our tour!

Kevin: I just want to clear something up . . . I just read the *Rolling Stone* article, and there's something in there that seems like a quote from one of us . . . that is absolutely not true . . . about the way the album was named . . . we named it *Black & Blue* because we were bruised about the way we were treated or something. We named the album *Black & Blue* for a silly reason – we couldn't think of anything else to name it, and we were doing a photo shoot, and we were all dressed in black in front of a blue background, and Brian said let's call the album *Black & Blue* and it stuck like that. If other people want to try and put deeper meaning into that, that's fine, but it didn't come from us – that's not a quote from us.

Q: How do you look at security now that you're super huge?

AJ: I think we've gotten to the point now where you still don't realize how many wackos there are out there, and there are always people who might try to do something wacky . . . stalkers, people who might try to end your career short. We've got an excellent security staff with us, and they've been with us for the last few years, they keep us as safe as they possibly can. There's only so much they can do. But when we're home at our domiciles, by ourselves – you just have to be careful where you go, picky and choosy about what you do – you don't go places where you might get jumped, you know. You have to call the restaurant ahead of time, I'm coming with my family, can you give me a private room. Call movie theaters – we almost have to do our own advance work. Book shopping – Brian will do it at 3:00 in the morning.

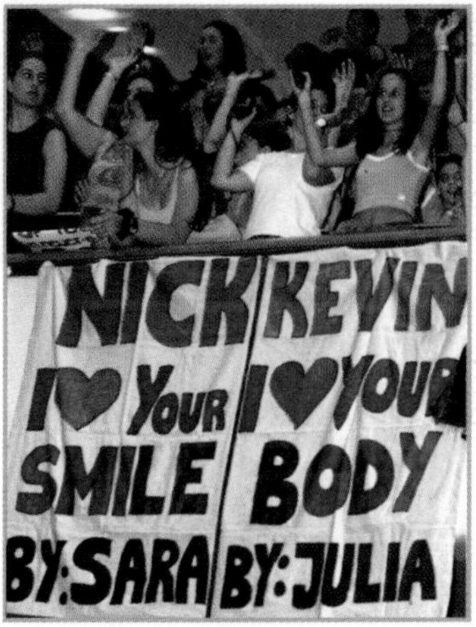

AP/WWP

Fans in Germany display signs for their favorite members of the band.

Nick: AJ just goes out!

AJ: I don't care! I go anywhere!

Howie: We want to be close to our fans out there—but there are certain times when we have to take certain measures.

Q: How do you feel you guys have grown personally and professionally?

Brian: Well, we've all grown some facial hair!

AJ: I think musically . . . we've grown – probably the most. Obviously, we're all grown up, we're all getting older, Kevin just had a birthday. But on this album especially – we went down to the Bahamas, just us five, in May or June – and we didn't know how it was going to go, if we were going to kill each other or work together. Basically, we came up with nine songs that we wrote together, two of which are on the *Black & Blue* album, and just the fact that we wrote the songs on this album shows a lot of growth for us. There's a lot more inspiration and a lot more participation from our side, and musically, production-wise. And the same thing with our tours, we're trying to grow slowly with our fans, and as a group. We're taking it step by step. We're all getting older –

AP/WWP

AJ reaches out and touches a fan during a 1997 tour stop in Bonn, Germany.

Howie: I decided to let my hair down for this album!

Q: What about fighting? Do you guys fight a lot?

Kevin: We sure do!

Q: Should you call yourselves the Backstreet Men? How has this album evolved?

Howie: We'll always be the Backstreet Boys, because boys – it means we're just friends – there's the Beach Boys, and they never changed their name to the Beach Men! And I mean, from the last album to this album, we definitely grew a lot, like AJ was saying. Personally as well as musically – and we feel like our sound is maturing, and we'd like to keep evolving with our fans. We want to make better music for each album to come.

Q: What was the best part of being on the plane around the world?

Nick: The plane! The plane!

Howie: We could only afford it for four days!

Brian: Actually, it was a very spoiling experience. Traveling that way was kind of nice, it was relaxing. We did some meet-and-greets and press conferences, we actually carried contest winners on the plane with us, to each country, which was kind of exciting. We brought two fans from Stockholm when we got started, and they flew to Tokyo with us. To see their eyes on the plane, and to see them look around, it's a cool experience. Because – it's not that we're used to it! I will never get used to a plane like that, and I think I can speak for everyone else – Howie was right, we could definitely only afford it for four days!

Anders Wiklund/Scanpix/Retna

The Boys pose in front of the luxury jet they chartered for their worldwide tour.

Q: You were supposed to do a South America concert but cancelled. Why?

Howie: That was a charity show for my Lupus foundation, and with everything going on with Backstreet Boys schedules, everyday it's constantly changing, and the reason I had to cancel was because we had to finish the album – that was very important to us. And I made a pledge, and an announcement that I want to come back to South America, because Lupus – it affects many members of the Latin community, and a major goal of mine is to take concerts all over South America – I was lucky to get to go to Puerto Rico and Argentina this time around. That's why – we were supposed to go to Caracas on the last part of this six-continent tour, but unfortunately with our time, trying to get back to America to be here for our album release, we had to pick a country that was a little bit closer, and that's why we picked Brazil. We're planning to come to Venezuela on the South America part of our tour, and we're very excited about that.

AP/WWP

Howie meets with reporters at a Lupus 2000 benefit concert he organized in memory of his sister, who died from the disease.

Kevin: As far as coming to places only when we need them, it's been four years since we've been to Tokyo or Australia. We've never been to South Africa and we've never been to Rio.

The most important part of what we were doing for this promotion is that, for the last album, we promoted *Millennium* – we didn't do any international promotion. We were kind of selfish and we kind of stayed here in the U.S. and promoted the album. And as you can see, our fans are excited to have us here. We have so many fans all over the world, and it's hard to maintain a healthy lifestyle and maintain your mental sanity and your physical health and well-being, and also get around to seeing everyone who wants to see you.

We eventually toured in Argentina, and we've been to South America and done several dates down there. We've never taken our tour to Japan or Australia, and that's why with this *Black & Blue* world tour, it will first and foremost be a world tour – we will go to everywhere for the first time, and that's important to us.

Reuters/Paulo Whitaker/Corbis

Brazilian fans cheer for their favorite band before a concert on the Backstreet Boys' *Black & Blue* world tour.

Brian: You see those pictures that are numbers, that are blurred – like if someone was taking a picture of Times Square, and you see cabs and people walking, and everything is blurred. The first one third of the picture would be nothing but blur, the middle would be entirely in focus, and the end would be a blur again – that's kind of how our careers have been until this point. And the middle symbolizes the *Black & Blue* record – it's probably been the most focused we've been as a group, and what's to come – we let that be. ♪

CD Spotlight

Everyone knows that the Backstreet Boys were a huge hit in just about every part of the world *except* the United States when they first started out. After touring Europe and Asia, when the Backstreet Boys returned to the United States in 1997, they felt like strangers in their own land. They were one of the most popular groups in the world – and almost totally unknown at home. That, however, was about to change.

The Backstreet Boys Come To The United States

> "Writing and producing — those are goals for us. In the beginning, we were just vocalists. I mean, we'd written songs, but the quality of the songs we were writing weren't up to par with the people we were working with. We've learned a lot from all these great writers and producers we've worked with."
>
> — Howie, on how the Backstreet Boys have developed their craft. ♪

The initial reviews of the Backstreet Boys' debut U.S. singles really didn't provide any notice that the quintet would become the next big thing in American music. *USA Today,* commenting on the Backstreet Boys' return to their homeland, said, "They've got their work cut out for them." Another critic chimed in, "It's going to be tough for them. It's a different market here."

But as they've gone on to prove repeatedly throughout their career, the Backstreet Boys really did not need to get the approval of the critics. The outstanding quality of Their songs spoke for themselves. When "Quit Playing Games (With My Heart)" was released in July 1997, it shot onto the charts.

On August 12 of that year, the Backstreet Boys' first American CD, the self-titled *Backstreet Boys,* hit stores, featuring a combination of tracks from their European releases, along with several all-new songs. It was tremendously popular, and stores across the country quickly sold out of the disc. Even critics had to take back their dire predictions once they heard the band's infectious, professional tunes.

BACKSTREET BOYS
1. We've Got It Goin' On
2. Quit Playing Games (With My Heart)
3. As Long As You Love Me
4. All I Have To Give
5. Anywhere For You
6. Hey, Mr. DJ (Keep Playin' This Song)
7. I'll Never Break Your Heart
8. Darlin'
9. Get Down (You're The One For Me)
10. Set Adrift On Memory Bliss
11. If You Want It To Be Good Girl (Get Yourself A Bad Boy)

"While many in the R&B camp convey soulfulness by moaning, groaning and contorting their voices in mock pain," said *PEOPLE* magazine, "the more pop-conscious Backstreet Boys sing like they're having a ball."

Nothing could be closer to the truth than that. The Backstreet Boys were genuinely excited about the opportunity to become superstars on their home turf.

"This is our home country," Howie related to the press, "and we've been waiting so long to come home. We took the backwards approach, going around the world and then coming back here. But I think, looking back on it all, it was a good decision. We wouldn't change anything, because we got the chance to really hone our craft and got a chance to see the world. I think a lot of artists who become

Larry Busacca/Retna

The guys pose for an early photo.

big over here, then go around the world – they just go briefly, in and out, just for the show. We got the chance to actually go into these countries and actually see the culture, visit some of the really small cities. The people there really appreciated us."

AJ added, "I think the second time is a charm for us instead of the third time. I think we are going to be more legit this time. Better music." In terms of the reason that the debut CD connected so readily, he added, "I think it's the versatility of the album. We cover every ground of every age group of every race. We don't just specifically want to cover one type of people. We want everyone to love our music. That is what the Backstreet Boys is all about. Family, fun and stuff like that."

And it didn't hurt that the songs had proven track records in Europe. "This album has five of our singles that we released in Europe," Kevin said. "Since we released our album in Europe, lots of producers became interested in working with us and we have gotten some really great new songs added. So it's like the best of what we've been doing for the past two years. We are really excited."

Working Vacation

The Backstreet Boys tried a different approach when recording *Black & Blue.* They worked in a secluded studio in the Bahamas, where they spent about three intensive weeks putting 100% effort into creating their CD. ♪

The Dawn Of Millennium

And so were their millions of fans, who wondered what would be next from the guys. The

MILLENNIUM
1. Larger Than Life
2. I Want It That Way
3. Show Me The Meaning Of Being Lonely
4. It's Gotta Be You
5. I Need You Tonight
6. Don't Want You Back
7. Don't Wanna Lose You Now
8. The One
9. Back To Your Heart
10. Spanish Eyes
11. No One Else Comes Close
12. The Perfect Fan

answer to that particular question would come soon enough when "I Want It That Way" – the first single from their second American CD, *Millennium* – was released and quickly became the #1-requested song on radio stations across the country.

Of course, the response wasn't really surprising to anyone who's followed the Backstreet Boys phenomenon. Fans were climbing the walls for months in anticipation of the May 18, 1999, release of the disc. After all, they knew *Millennium* was going to be something special. The idea was that this would be the CD that would allow the Backstreet Boys to step forward and show the world that they were more than just pretty voices; that they had a role in their own destiny.

"On the first CD," Kevin said, "most of the stuff was done by writers and producers that our record company arranged. Now we're adding a little more of our own music into the mix."

It's that mature, realistic attitude that has made the Backstreet Boys such stars. Says Jive executive Jeffrey Fenster of *Millennium,* "It's one of those good situations where everyone says, 'We're going to show growth in our next album, but we're going to do it in the smart and gradual way.'"

As Kevin related to *World Of Sound,* "We were just trying to make good music that we loved to sing and perform and that our fans would love. We feel like we've grown on this album. It's deeper lyrically, but it's not over our young fans' heads. We're just trying to keep with the times in order to stay in the pop music scene. 'Pop' is short for 'popular,' so we're just trying to keep evolving with the times, just like Madonna did, just like Janet and Michael Jackson, so we'll have a long career."

The band poses with John Lebbad, director of marketing for Sears (third from left), before kicking off their *Millennium* tour.

The members of the band agree that life experiences have had a lot to do with the fact that the lyrics on the CD are a bit deeper than they had been on their first effort. Among the "maturing" factors had been Brian's heart surgery and the death of Howie's sister. That influence can be seen on "Show Me The Meaning Of Being Lonely," easily the most touching ballad on the CD.

Howie pointed out that it wasn't as though the group was trying to be a more grown-up version of itself. It was a much more natural process than that. "We were just trying to set new goals and challenges for ourselves musically," he said. "We couldn't make the same album as the first one. If it attracts an older audience as well as our younger fans, all the better."

For his part, Brian believes that the first CD more or less made an easy path for their second to be so successful. "The first album set us apart from everyone else," he mused to *Teen People.* "We're thankful we came first, but everybody that came behind us . . . we did a lot of opening doors [for them]. I think we'll continue to do that with this album. We're in a great situation. As artists, we had time to sit and focus on what got us to where we're at today, and that's working hard in the studio and making good songs."

Turning Black & Blue

Good sales don't hurt either. In its debut week, *Millennium* obliterated all previous sales records by moving 1.1 million copies. This created great pressure on the Backstreet Boys – imposed more so by the media than themselves – for their next CD to sell even better. Their third American CD, *Black & Blue,* was released in November 2000.

BLACK & BLUE

1. The Call
2. Shape Of My Heart
3. Get Another Boyfriend
4. Shining Star
5. I Promise You (With Everything I Am)
6. The Answer To Our Life
7. Everyone
8. More Than That
9. Time
10. Not For Me
11. Yes I Will
12. It's True
13. What Makes You Different (Makes You Beautiful)
14. How Did I Fall In Love With You

The Backstreet Boys had two goals with the new CD: to move forward musically yet again; to take their past success and use it to pave the way to the future without completely duplicating it.

So exactly what did come out? On its release, *Black & Blue* knocked the Beatles' *#1* disc off the top of the *Billboard* charts – although the Beatles would come back to top the charts a couple of weeks later.

Musically, the guys are feeling quite thrilled with what they were able to accomplish.

"We're constantly trying to strive to be

better at our craft," said Howie, "and with each album, not just settling with one or two potential singles, and the rest just album fillers. Our goal is to try to make every song a potential single and make it the best. *Millennium* is a very special thing that came across, and it's almost like Michael Jackson's *Thriller* – sometimes you get this big, big album, and it's like, where do you go from there? But this album was more of a growth for us. I think it crosses over to everyone. Hopefully someone will find at least one song they can really identify with."

The guys are all bundled up for the annual Jingle Ball at Madison Square Garden in New York City.

The real question on people's minds, however, is how they came up with a title like *Black & Blue*. Part of it, they've explained, has to do with what they've been through in terms of personal issues and business ones, such as the lawsuit with Louis J. Pearlman. Like the title 'NSYNC chose for their first CD without Pearlman – *No Strings Attached* – this one was symbolic as well (though they've occasionally denied the symbolism).

Record-Breaking Success

Black & Blue sold more than 5 million copies in its first week of worldwide release – setting a new international sales record! ♪

"We scoured our brains and finally said, 'Let's do a color,'" Howie explained. "'Let's do a cool color,' but the cool colors were already taken – the white album! We didn't want to go with pink or fuchsia. So we went in to do the album cover and we were wearing black for one outfit and we were standing in front of the blue background, and we thought, 'Oh!

Black and blue! Cool!' It has a lot of hidden meaning. Groups like us, we always get titles like 'boy band,' 'bubble gum,' 'popcorn' – all these punches because of the type of group that we are, and we thought, we've been through all that and we're still standing. We're still making music."

"We've kind of grown in a way," added Brian, "that we can present something the way we want to present it, and it was the kind of thing where the album cover is half black and half blue, and there's no picture. The picture is on the back – we wanted to go more adult, more artsy, something that kind of jumps out at you when you're in the record store and you see it on the shelf."

Phil Loftus/Scanpix/Flash/Retna

The Backstreet Boys answer questions at a press conference in Sweden for the MTV Europe Awards.

Obviously the experiment worked, as *Black & Blue* has flown off of the shelves, causing fans to already start asking the inevitable question: what's next? The Backstreet Boys, a group always determined to keep their fans guessing, will provide the answer within the next year. In the meantime, there's a tour to think about. ♪

Topping The Charts

AJ, Brian, Howie, Kevin and Nick would be the first ones to tell you that despite how easy it looked, their road to success was well-traveled and hard-earned.

1995

The Backstreet Boys' first attempt at getting the U.S. public to buy their music wasn't very successful. Their first single, "We've Got It Goin' On," was released in the United States in **October**, debuting at #95. The highest rank it would achieve would be #69, which it reached in **December**. In total, the single spent 20 weeks on the *Billboard* charts.

In Europe, however, the situation was vastly different, as the guys had already established a fan base there. In Germany, the single made it to the top ten.

1997

Despite their European success, the Backstreet Boys didn't make a dent in the United States for another couple of years. Then, finally, in **August**, their record label, Jive, issued the Backstreet Boys' self-titled CD, which debuted on the *Billboard* charts at #29.

The first song off the CD was "Quit Playin' Games (With My Heart)." That single scored significantly better than the one that came before it two years earlier. The new song debuted at #24 in

AP/WWP

From left to right, Brian, Howie, Nick, Kevin and AJ perform for a televised concert in Germany in 1999.

June and peaked at #2 in **September**. Ultimately, it would spend 43 weeks on the charts.

The guys strut their stuff on stage in New York.

1998

The next single off the *Backstreet Boys* CD would eventually reach its highest chart ranking in **January**. It would go on to spend an astounding 133 weeks – more than 2 years! – on the charts, eventually selling 13 million copies.

The *Backstreet Boys* next single, "Everybody (Backstreet's Back)," like its predecessor, made its debut at #24 in **April**, peaking at #4 in **May**. Where it fell short of "Quit Playin' Games (With My Heart)" is that it only spent 22 weeks on the charts, nearly half as long as "Quit Playin' Games . . ."

The third single, "I'll Never Break Your Heart," debuted at #35 in **December**. That debut slot was the highest chart ranking that song would achieve, although it held a place on the *Billboard* charts for a respectable 21 weeks.

1999

The final single from the Backstreet Boys' self-titled U.S. debut album was "All I Have To Give." Released in **January**, it zoomed up to #5 just one week later – demonstrating the growing popularity of the band – and spent 21 weeks on the charts – just like the song that came before it.

The Backstreet Boys' follow-up CD to their phenomenal U.S. debut was *Millennium,* which was issued in **June** and debuted in the #1 position, where it remained for 10 straight weeks. The CD itself – which would go on to sell 13 million copies – spent 91 weeks on the charts.

It's True

"It's True," a song from their Black & Blue album, can also be found on three CDs available exclusively at Burger King. ♪

The first single to be released from *Millennium* was "I Want It That Way." The ballad made its debut on the *Billboard* charts in **April** at #72. By **June**, it managed to reach #6, and stayed on the charts for an impressive 31 weeks.

In a somewhat controversial move, Jive Records waited five long months to issue a follow-up single to "I Want It That Way." "Larger Than Life" debuted at #70 in **September**. Surprisingly, its highest charting position was #25, which it attained in **November**. It spent 19 weeks on the charts.

2000

However, the Backstreet Boys rebounded easily from the poor showing of "Larger Than Life." "Show Me The Meaning Of Being Lonely," arguably the strongest song on *Millennium,* was issued as

Dave Hogan/ImageDirect

The Backstreet Boys rehearse before heading on stage.

a single in **January** at #74. By the time **March** rolled around, the song had moved up to #6, and would ultimately go on to spend 24 weeks on the charts.

The final track to be issued as a single from *Millennium* was "The One." That song made its debut in **May** at #58. It would only make it up to #30, which it did in **July**. "The One" became the worst-performing Backstreet Boys song to date, spending a mere 15 weeks on the charts.

Brian performs some well-rehearsed dance moves.

AP/WWP

The Backstreet Boys' most recent album, *Black & Blue,* debuted at #1 in **December**, which is where it stayed for two weeks before being knocked off the top perch by the Beatles *#1*.

Black & Blue gave birth to its first single, "Shape of My Heart," in **October**. By **December**, it had made it to #9 and spent 20 weeks on the charts.

2001

At press time, "The Call" – the most recent Backstreet Boys single – was released in **February** and was charted at #56, while *Black & Blue* had spent 12 weeks on the charts and had sold more than eight million copies. ♪

Proven To Be #1

The Backstreet Boys' singles aren't the only thing hitting the top of the charts! The band holds the record for having the most number of videos (eight) reach #1 on MTV's *TRL* video countdown. ♪

The Backstreet Project

Dotcoms are falling prey to fiscal villainy! Chaos rules! Who will save Internet entertainment? Would you believe, the Backstreet Boys?

That's right. The Backstreet Boys have been transformed into superheros, both on the pages of comic books (found at BSB concerts or for sale on the Internet) and in action on the Internet.

While the Backstreet Boys have gathered an incredible amount of musical experience over the past few years, little can compare to this newest version of the band. Created by Stan Lee – who brought the world such incredible comic book characters as Spider-Man, the Fantastic Four and the X-Men – and Nick Carter, this comic book adventure offers a tale in which a female alien lands on Earth ahead of a full-blown invasion force. The alien manages to pass on magical amulets to the five Backstreet Boys. As a result, the band members are endowed with cool costumes and superpowers so that they will be able to defend Earth from the approaching space army and party down when they're through.

From Boys To Supermen

Brian, whose chiseled good looks and light-colored hair are reflected in his comic book character, is the first to discover his newfound power when he jumps out of the way of a giant robot. Brian, who is an avid basket-

James Smeal/Galella LTD

Brian and Kevin at the Billboard Music Awards, and their Backstreet Project alter egos.

ball player in real life, finds that he can also conjure up a mystic ball of energy that looks a lot like a basketball.

Kevin's comic book character is immediately recognizable from his dark good looks and defined features. Sporting spiky hair (the real Kevin's hair has since grown longer), Kevin discovers that he has superhuman physical and mental strength that even allows him to lift a spaceship out of a nearby lake and then fly it! Not only that, but he gets to wear an ultra-hip red suit of armor that protects him when battling the bad guys.

Jim Smeal/Galella LTD

AJ and Howie (at the American Music Awards) look pretty similar to the comic book AJ and Howie.

AJ, looking cool (as always) in dark sunglasses, a trench coat and his trademark earrings, is the world's best marksman, able to use any weapon that he gets his hands on – including a variety of advanced weapons unlike any ever before seen on Earth.

The animated Howie sports a ponytail, goatee and large earring, not unlike the real Howie. When he puts on his amulet, he finds himself in a blue and gold robe, and realizes that he has telepathic powers, which allow him to project 3-D illusions of anything he wants.

Nick may be the baby of the group, but he sure works just as hard as the other guys in saving the planet! This blond-haired cutie shares his wholesome good looks with the real-life Nick Carter. When he puts on the magic amulet, the comic book version of Nick is rewarded with an uncanny ability to fix things and is also given

Henry Lamb/Galella LTD

The Backstreet Project was Nick's idea. His comic book image is in the inset.

incredible Ninja powers that make him the world's best martial artist.

Nick's Love Of Comics

The origin of the Backstreet Project can be traced to Nick's lifelong fascination with comic books, first as a reader and then in his long-held dream of turning the band into comic book heroes. At about the same time, Stan Lee decided to start up his own Internet company, which he hoped would offer a number of features, most notably animated comic book "webisodes" running three to five minutes each. Stan read Nick's proposal – which had the band battling aliens on Mars – and was intrigued enough by it to suggest a collaboration. The idea was to create a comic book that would be sold only on the Internet and at Backstreet Boys shows and then to create webisodes that would expand on the comic.

What's A "Webisode"?

"Webisode" is the combination of "world wide web" and "episode." It's used when talking about anything that's presented in a serialized form on the Internet. So, when you're looking for the latest Backstreet Project story on the Internet, you're looking for their latest webisode. ♪

Nick and Stan had the concept for the idea, which Bryce Zabel, a television writer/producer employed by Stan Lee Media, turned into an outline for a story. From there, the outline was turned into a series of sketches by artist Ruben Martinez, for which Stan then wrote the dialogue. "I gave the bones to the story," Zabel said. "Stan and Nick had a concept of powers and the large framework, and I put the flesh on that story.

"There was a strategic alliance struck between the Backstreet Boys and Stan Lee

The cover of The Backstreet Project's first comic book.

Media to do the comic book as a way of trying to reach out to an audience that the Backstreet Boys might not have had," says Zabel. "The Backstreet Boys typically have had a largely female audience – almost exclusively female audience. Yet the comic book world is largely male. So the theory went that if you did a comic book with the Backstreet Boys, everybody wins. Stan Lee gets more women logging on to Stan Lee Media, which they needed, and the Backstreet Boys get more guys basically tuning in to their music, which they needed. And everybody wins. I think that was the theory, that it would allow two audiences to kind of co-mingle. That's why they decided to go ahead with it."

Alakazam! A Comic Book

On the surface, it would seem that turning the Backstreet Boys into a comic book wouldn't require much work, but, according to Zabel, it was more challenging than one might think.

Pay Them A Visit

Log onto the The Backstreet Project at its official website, www.backstreetproject.com or through its parent site, www.stanleemedia.com. ♪

"Anybody can be given superpowers," he says. "You can pick a guy out of the phone book and say, 'Okay, let's do a story about this guy or woman getting superpowers.' So that part is easy enough. The biggest storytelling problem is that you have five characters, all of whom have superpowers and the powers all need to add up at certain key points to victory

"They have to fight crime by day, because at night they're booked. Someone has to keep the world safe during the daytime."

— Backstreet Project writer Bryce Zabel, on when the super hero Backstreet Boys might perform their out-of-this-world duties. ♪

over the bad guys. And everybody needs to get a semi-equal amount of 'screen' time, superpower time and dialogue time. So the biggest challenge in crafting a story and adding the dialogue for one of these types of comics is just balancing everybody's involvement. It's like writing *The Avengers* or *The X-Men.* There are a lot of characters and they need to DO something. They can't just stand around and comment on the other guy. So that's the hardest part."

Super Popular Superheroes

The Backstreet Project has been an enormous success, the comic having gone into a second printing. But what, exactly, is the reason that it's touched a chord with people?

"I think the appeal for the fans is when you're a fan of someone or something, you always love to see it in different forms, because that's the joy of the whole thing," Zabel offers. "So here's the expression of the Backstreet Boys' personality in a wholly different form and it's fun. I think that's why the comic book has sold so well in these venues, because it adds a whole new way of looking at the Backstreet Boys that's just fun."

And lucrative as well. Last summer Burger King launched a major Backstreet Boys promotion designed to let fans know that their third album – *Black & Blue* – was coming, and to fill them in on the Backstreet Project. Fans buying kid's meals were given action figures of each of the guys dressed in their superhero outfits. Over 40 million action figures were given away. Peter Paul, a co-founder of Stan Lee Media, said, "This is the largest off-line promotion ever for an on-line event."

Would you expect anything less from the Backstreet Boys? ♪

What The Critics Say About The Backstreet Boys

While the Backstreet Boys have touched the hearts and imaginations of people around the world – and their music is viewed as a phenomenal success just about anywhere you can travel – the critics haven't always been as supportive of the group as their fans have been.

Like many start-up bands, their self-titled debut album was barely acknowledged critically. However, the band's many singles began to dominate the airwaves and their success soon became undeniable. By the time of *Millennium*'s release, the media were much more willing to provide a thorough examination of what was offered up by the band. This was even more true with the recent release of *Black & Blue*.

AP/WWP

The Backstreet Boys celebrate the success of their debut album at a press conference in 1997.

The First CD: Backstreet Boys

When the *Backstreet Boys* CD was released in 1997, most critics initially wrote the band off as the latest in a long line of bubble-gum pop. They might have a few hits, but their fame would be fleeting, many said.

Billboard was one reviewer that complimented the Backstreet Boys' sound, but also compared them to others: "Young quintet debuts with an album that both lives up to its billing as a vocal-oriented pop sensation and bears out comparisons to New Kids On The Block . . . [Certain] cuts showcase the Boys' gift for delivering lethally catchy pop gems. Other cuts . . . suggest slightly more sophisticated musical leanings. Already a smash at pop radio, the group stands to benefit from a climate that has made superstars out of Spice Girls and Hanson."

Referencing the group's early release overseas, *All Music Guide* added, "The Backstreet Boys' eponymous debut album was released in America nearly a full year after its original European release, and the wait proved to be a blessing in disguise. In that year, light dance-pop – such as the Spice Girls and Hanson – returned to the top of the American charts, paving the way for the frothy pleasures of the Backstreet Boys . . . Each of the singles, plus a handful of album tracks, are potent combinations of professional hooks and personal charm that make *Backstreet Boys* a thoroughly enjoyable affair."

The Second CD: Millennium

It was 1999 – two years before the Backstreet Boys' eagerly awaited second release arrived – and critics had much to say about the group's sophomore effort.

Seventeen magazine commented on the similarities between the band's two discs and gave the band a relatively positive review – with a warning. "If you thought they were cheesier than a plate of nachos," the magazine began, "*Millennium* probably isn't for you. The upbeat tracks . . . are much hotter than the slow jams, since the Boys excel at shaking those rumps. They were the first, and they still stand apart from the crowd. That alone makes *Millennium* worth at least one listen while you're wandering around the record store."

Henry Lamb/Ron Galella LTD

Howie, Kevin, Nick, AJ and Brian (left to right) publicize their *Millennium* tour at Studio 54 in New York City.

"The Boys play it as well or better than any other of their peers," agreed the *Chicago Tribune*. " . . . the Backstreet gang makes blue-eyed soul of engaging subtlety."

Rolling Stone was just as enthusiastic, noting, "Prefabricated, too pretty, suspiciously well choreographed – such objects to the Backstreet Boys wither in the face of singles like the undeniable 'Everybody (Backstreet's Back)' and the sweet soar of 'I'll Never Break Your Heart.' The Boys follow-up their tenfold-platinum debut with an album filled with examples of their forte: New Jack doo-wop and lyrically trivial, rhythmically insistent funk lite . . . The ballad 'Show Me The Meaning Of Being Lonely' digs its melodic claws into your skull on the first listen – it's the swooniest blending of the five vocalists' timbres to date, and mighty pretty besides."

Are You Ready?

When the Backstreet Boys formed in 1993, the United States wasn't ready for them. Their first record label, Mercury, dropped them before they even recorded a song. It was their second label, Jive, that recognized that the world was begging for their soulful pop. Look how far they've come! ♪

Perhaps MTV summed up the album best. "*Millennium* is all about giving the people what they want . . . This record didn't need to be better. It didn't need word-of-mouth. It didn't need critical approval. It just needed to be the Backstreet Boys doing what the Backstreet Boys do best. And what they're best at is making relentlessly upbeat pop music that people want to listen to."

John Gladwin/Retna

The guys look prepare to blast into the "millennium" at a recent concert.

The Third CD: Black & Blue

But, perhaps to prove that pop music wasn't their only forte (as the MTV review suggested), the Backstreet Boys took a somewhat different tone for their third album in 2000 – and it didn't go unnoticed by critics.

"The Boys mature into Backstreet Men before our ears," was the way *Entertainment Weekly* summed up the change.

Wrote *Billboard*, "The act that helped start the ever-hot teen-pop movement returns with a collection shrewdly designed to affirm the Boys' superior status as popmeisters while valiantly striving to prove their potential for adult durability . . .[with] several wonderfully engaging slow jams."

"*Black & Blue* finds the Boys more or less ceding the world of high-energy dance pop," wrote *Wall Of Sound,* "and instead putting the spotlight on slower, quieter songs that serve as better showcases for their particular vocal blend. And that is, indeed, where the Boys shine best on *Black & Blue*. While the group . . . dutifully troops its way through by-the-numbers up-tempo fare . . . the ballads about hearts that soar, break and bruise easily are by and large more fully realized and passionately rendered . . . This may be one of the signs of maturity; rather than delving toward the cutting edge"

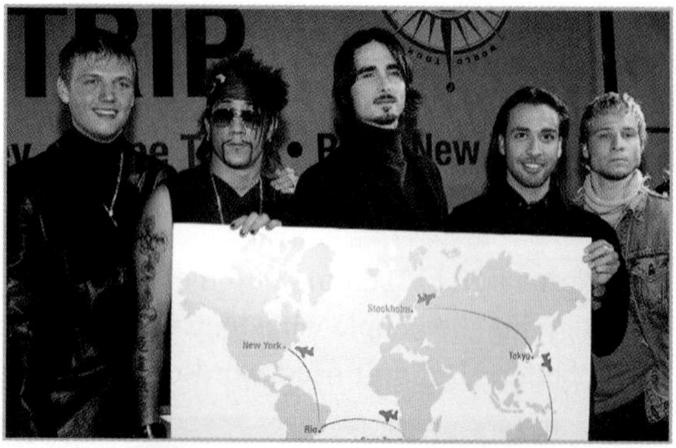

Dave Hogan/MP/ImageDirect

The Boys describe their planned route for their six-continents-in-four-days promotional tour.

Are the Backstreet Boys getting softer as they get older? Or did they just want to prove that their talent extends beyond traditional pop? Now proven masters of both pop and contemporary music, the critics are surely anticipating what this band will do next! ♪

Larger Than Life: Videos By The Backstreet Boys

> **"Get Down"**
>
> Only released in Europe, this video is quite fun as the Backstreet Boys dance and sing inside a disco glitter ball, surrounded by screens of dancers. There are some very cool visuals as the guys seem to be on a floating platform in the center of the ball as they dance energetically. The song makes you want to do what they tell you — get down! ♪

One of the things, aside from their status as hard-core hotties, that has made the Backstreet Boys so successful is their music videos. Listening to the music is great, but watching them in action makes the whole Backstreet Boys experience that much more entertaining.

"We've Got It Going On"

This video gives Backstreet Boys fans a treat – seeing the Boys looking very much like boys with their baby faces at the very beginning of their career. The guys dance, play pool, lift weights and dance as they sing their own praises to a cute beat. Their dance moves are a little rough – you can tell that they haven't really found their look yet. The song and video went nowhere in the United States, but began the band's climb as pop icons.

AP/WWP

The guys practice their moves during a rehearsal in Austria in 1996.

"Quit Playing Games (With My Heart)"

In "Quit Playing Games (With My Heart)," we're given the same handsome faces – but quite a bit younger! With the word "Games" being in the title, we're given the Backstreet Boys on a basketball court. The video offers the standard romantic images of the guys in their flowing shirts, kneeling in the rain, baring their washboard fronts. As an early work, it's fine. But thankfully, the band moved on to better videos from here.

"All I Have To Give"

This video is a remake of the old Full Force ballad, which the Backstreet Boys expertly cover. Nigel Dick, who has also worked with Britney Spears, Christina Aguilera and many others, is behind the camera, and produces sweet images, some in slow motion, along with a nice visual play of light and shadow. The Backstreet Boys are as gorgeous as ever and so heartfelt that you can't help but melt over their words and music, as well as their overwhelming eyes and "to-die-for" smiles.

"I'll Never Break Your Heart": Version 2

The European video for this song is far superior to the American version as the guys goof around a ski lodge with the Alps as their background. The video has them playing in the snow, a fresh break from studio-bound sites. The video moves along nicely as the power of the tune increases, winding up with all romantic entanglements sewn up just in time for sledding. ♪

"As Long As You Love Me"

Nigel Dick also built a very charming video around this sweet and uplifting song. The Backstreet Boys try to impress a gaggle of serious career women with different costumes and hair styles before turning the tables on the femme professionals by having the ladies pose for the band. The guys are very charming in their close-ups and funny in their outrageous clothes. Expert choreography enhances the mood of both the video and the song, especially in the premiere of the now-legendary "chair dance" that the band

Making The Video

The Backstreet Boys' home video, All Access, has a wonderful behind-the-scenes documentary about the making of "Everybody," including interesting "how-they-did-it" details. ♪

re-creates in concert as flawlessly as they did in the music video. This song is one of the band's best ballads, and translates into a nice, romantic video.

"Everybody (Backstreet's Back)"

If anyone ever doubted that the Backstreet Boys could rock, that doubt was dispelled with "Everybody (Backstreet's Back)." The song's infectious beat and the video's incredible dancing and stunning production values took the Backstreet Boys to the top all around the world.

The video is an expert mixture of fun and fancy: Nick's swaying Mummy, Howie's dark Dracula, Brian's fiercely tumbling Wolfman, Kevin's subdued Hyde and AJ's masterful Phantom keep things visually lively with the cool computer effects and the stunning sets and costumes adding to the fun. The choreography is a great complement to the beat, making it almost impossible to watch the video sitting down. And two of the best parts in the

AP/WWP

The guys put on a power-packed performance at the 1998 Vina del Mar Song Festival in Chile.

entire production are at the beginning and end when the Backstreet Boys are joined by bus driver Antonio Vargas to take refuge in the spooky hotel, only to wake up from their communal nightmare to offer screams at the sight of the undead Antonio. It remains one of their best videos on all levels.

"Larger Than Life"

"Larger Than Life" is certainly larger than most videos in both scope and cost. This sci-fi–inspired work includes stunning costumes, great dancing and remarkable special effects in what has to be one of the most extravagant videos of all time.

Within its space-fighter narrative, the video is reminiscent of the *Lost In Space* movie that had come out that previous spring. The video is visually stunning, with an anti-gravity skateboard right out of *Back To The Future II*.

"The One"

Co-directed by the group's very own Kevin Richardson, "The One" is a fast and flashy concert clip video. There are some great eye-catching shots in this video, but they pass so quickly that they are lost. The ultimate power the video might have had is lessened by its own speed.

"Show Me The Meaning Of Being Lonely"

This is, to date, one of the most personal videos and songs the Backstreet Boys have ever filmed/recorded. They each face their pasts in the video, walking the streets of New York City, giving full vent to usually hidden, very private feelings. While art is found in such works, be

Kevin Hively/L.A. Times/Retna

Nick, Howie and Brian in action.

warned, as the video is quite a downer, leaving you with a feeling that is so unlike what you expect from the Backstreet Boys.

"The Shape Of My Heart"

This ballad has a pleasing sound – sweet and bitter at the same time. When captured on video, the song adds an extra dramatic line in the emotional aura of an empty theater. The Backstreet Boys have grown up, and are even more handsome than ever. They seem a lot more comfortable acting in this story, compared to some of their earlier efforts. It's a crisply shot video, and the song is earnest without being sappy. It's one of their better videos.

The guys strike a pose for the camera.
Larry Busacca/Retna

The entire Backstreet Boys music video collection ought to be released on home video or DVD, shown chronologically, so fans can see a band and five talented young men grow from simple pop beginnings to the R&B masters they are today. While not every one of their videos is a winner, in such a gathering they would be a fun and fascinating gathering of works that detail the creative challenges of one of the most beloved musical acts in the world. ♪

"I'd Go Anywhere For You"

Available on Backstreet Boys: The Video, "I'd Go Anywhere For You" is another early work that wasn't released in the United States. It's basically the Backstreet Boys on the beach, having fun while surrounded by local beauties. This predictable video is not one of their best, just one of their earliest. ♪

BSB On TV

Can't get enough of the Backstreet Boys? Never fear – by turning on your TV you can see them every day! Whether it's their latest video, a live interview or performance or just goofing around, the Backstreet Boys can almost always be found somewhere on your TV dial! Here's a look at some of the band's many television highlights over the years.

BSB And The Teen Witch

The Backstreet Boys put their musical talents to use during a "battle of the bands," on an episode of *Sabrina The Teenage Witch.* During the episode, Sabrina uses a potion to make her friends more musically inclined – but little does she know just how much competition she is up against!

Live From New York!

The Backstreet Boys were featured as musical guests on *Saturday Night Live* on May 15, 1999. This show was a special one – not only because they blew the audience away with an a cappella version of "All I Have To Give," but because Howie appeared as himself in one of the skits as well!

At Home With AJ

If AJ is your favorite Backstreet Boy, then you won't want to have missed *MTV Cribs*, in which the group's craziest member opened up his five-bedroom home to viewers across the country! This show really gave you a glimpse of what it's like to chill with AJ, whether he's checking out his amazing hat collection, playing some tunes (with his feet!) on the piano or just lounging in his Olympic-sized swimming pool. Of course, he also couldn't help mugging with both girlfriend Amanda and his puppy!

The Backstreet Boys collaborated with MTV on another project – *MTV Diary*. This show is the closest you will probably get to actually hanging out with the band as they carry a camera around and film what it's like to a Backstreet Boy for a few days.

BSB At Your Fingertips

With eight VHS videos released so far, you always can watch the Backstreet Boys on TV – even when they're not on TV! These videos give you everything from unseen music video footage to actual concerts the Backstreet Boys have played, as well as an inside glimpse of what goes on behind the scenes. ♪

Backstreet In The News

They say that "the early bird gets the worm," and if you were up early from November 20-23, 2000, you got a treat as well! The Backstreet Boys appeared on a four-day special during this time on CBS' *The Early Show*. In addition to discussing their new album, how they got their start and their favorite movie picks with entertainment correspondent Mark McEwan, the boys played "Shape Of My Heart," as well as some old favorites from previous albums.

Bowled Over By BSB

Who could forget the Backstreet Boys' awesome rendition of the national anthem at Super Bowl XXXV on January 28, 2001? The group, who followed R&B legend Ray Charles singing "America The Beautiful," silenced the stadium with their heart-felt rendition of "The Star Spangled Banner"! As they finished their

AP/WWP

Nick, AJ, Brian, Kevin and Howie (left to right) sing "The Star Spangled Banner" as part of the Super Bowl XXXV opening ceremonies.

song, the elite Air Force group of "Thunderbirds" circled the stadium and the crowd cheered loudly. The day was extra-special for band member Nick Carter, a big football fan who told an interviewer, "The next day is my 21st birthday. I'm praying that all that comes together, because I want to have a really good birthday." Looks like he got his birthday wish! Way to go, guys!

Use The 50/50 Or Make The Call?

Which two members of the Backstreet Boys recently appeared on America's #1 game show, *Who Wants To Be A Millionaire?* Is that your final answer? If you guessed Howie and Kevin, then you're right! The duo appeared on a special "rock star" version of the popular quiz show in February of 2001. Even though neither of the guys made it into the game's "hot seat," they both had a great time and contributed to good causes – they each earned $32,000 for their favorite charities. ♪

Dave Hogan/MP/ImageDirect

Kevin and Howie (shown here on their world tour) took part in the rock stars version of *Who Wants To Be A Millionaire?* which aired in February 2001.

The Winner Is . . . The Backstreet Boys!

When they were first starting out, the Backstreet Boys didn't dare dream that their music would one day take the world by storm. Flash forward to today and not only do they make the girls swoon in every country on the map, but they've also collected enough awards, plaques and gold records to fill their entire tour bus – and then some!

European Awards

Success first came to the Backstreet Boys in Europe, where in 1995, less than a year after the release of their first single, the band nabbed Britain's Smash Hits Award for Best New Tour Act. And little did the Backstreet Boys know, this award was just the beginning!

Jean-Paul Pelissier/Reuters/Corbis

AJ and Howie accept a 2000 World Music Award for the world's best selling pop group.

Throughout the next few years, the Backstreet Boys would find themselves back overseas to accept honor after honor. Included in these awards were two voted on by viewers of VIVA, a German music television network similar to MTV: a Comet Award for Best Newcomers and the hefty title of Number One Boy Band.

But that's not all. The Backstreet Boys beat out popular groups like Oasis, the Spice Girls and Hanson to win the Select Award at the MTV Europe Awards two years in a row (1996 and 1997). The Select Award is the equivalent of the MTV Viewers' Choice Award in the United States – and the Backstreet Boys admitted that they were surprised to even be nominated in the company of such stellar acts. They followed up that win with an unheard-of five awards at

London's Smash Hits Awards show and two Best Group Awards from MTV Europe – in 1999 and 2000.

American Music Awards

In 1998, the band solidified their success in the United States with their first American Music Awards nomination in the Best New Group category. Although they didn't win, they would return two years later and take home the Best Rock Duo Or Group Award. Most recently, the Boys won the 2001 trophy for Favorite Pop Rock Band, Duo Or Group.

Billboard Awards

1998 presented the Boys with their first Billboard Award: for Best Group Album. They followed up the feat in 1999, when they took home four awards in the categories of Artist Of The Year, Album Of The Year (*Millennium*), Albums Artist Of The Year and Albums Artist Duo/Group Of The Year.

Steve Granitz/Retna

The guys celebrate their first Billboard Music Award in 1998.

Blockbuster Awards

The Backstreet Boys were named Favorite Pop Group and *Millennium* was named Favorite CD at the Blockbuster Entertainment Awards in June of 2000. In addition, the band has been nominated for Favorite Group Of The Year and Favorite Pop Group for 2001.

Grammy Awards

Although the band has yet to take home a prestigious Grammy Award, they have been recognized with five nominations: one in 1998 for Best New Group and five in 2000, for Record Of The Year, Album Of The Year, Pop Album Of The Year, Song Of The Year and Pop Song Of The Year. In 2001,they were nominated for a Best Pop Performance With Vocals Award for "Show Me The Meaning Of Being Lonely."

MTV Music Awards

In 1998, the Backstreet Boys won an award for Best Group Video with "Everybody (Backstreet's Back)." In 1999, they received the Viewers' Choice Award for "I Want It That Way."

Bill Davila/Retna

The Backstreet Boys pose with their Viewer's Choice Award at the 1999 MTV Video Music Awards.

Kid's Choice Award

Kids all over the United States voted "Everybody" their Favorite Song in 1999 and the Backstreet Boys their Favorite Musical Group in 2000. They are nominated again for Favorite Musical Group, but can they repeat the honor in 2001?

People's Choice Award

As if it wasn't obvious already, the band was officially named the people's choice for Favorite Musical Group Or Band in 2000.

We're sure that the awards will continue to roll in as long as the Backstreet Boys continue to work their music magic. ♪

On Tour With The Backstreet Boys

Music videos showing the Backstreet Boys dancing and singing are just fine, but nothing beats seeing them in a live performance!

Imagine the scene as you're in the stadium waiting for the show to start: the anticipation of fellow fans is so heavy that the air is thick enough to take a bite out of. You wonder if maybe – just maybe – the one of the Backstreet Boys might catch your eye from the stage. An electric chill runs through you then as your joy at being there is heightened while your heart beats just a little faster at the sight of those eyes locked on yours, even for just a second.

> "It's too bad the Backstreet Boys are branded with the dreaded label of boy band because they actually can sing."
>
> — Review of the Backstreet Boys Black & Blue tour in the Pittsburgh Post Gazette.

Sure beats *TRL.*

Galloping Through Europe

The Backstreet Boys' first touring experience came during November and December of 1995. Failing miserably to find a U.S. audience, their manager, Louis J. Pearlman, decided that their best bet would be to try to create a fan base overseas. To this end, they performed throughout the United Kingdom as part of the Smash Hits Roadshow.

Robert Spencer/Retna

Kevin plays to the audience during a concert in New York City.

Howie concentrates on his performance.

AP/WWP

Reasonably satisfied with this tour, the following winter, they hit Europe – hard! They focused on Germany, which was a country that had taken them close to its heart. As a result, their popularity continued to grow, as did their fan base.

By the summer of 1996, with a new album in the can (their self-titled debut), they began a tour of the Far East and Canada, drawing big crowds everywhere they went. By October, they moved on to South East Asia and Australia. A month later, they headlined a tour of 14 cities in mid-sized arenas and theaters in the United Kingdom and Europe.

By December of 1997, the Backstreet Boys finally came home to the United States. By this point, their popularity had grown tremendously in this country, and as a result they embarked on a tour that would take them throughout the United States.

Going To The Big Show

Needless to say, the Backstreet Boys are one of the busiest groups in the world, known and loved on every continent no matter how different the culture or language may be. Their tours are long stints across a country or around the world, and they fill auditoriums and city streets wherever they go. The chance to be in the audience of a Backstreet Boys concert is a high point for many Backstreet Boys fans, and they live for the thrill of seeing the band's actual bodies and hearing their live voices, rather than staring at images on a screen or listening to their voices on the radio.

And the best part of it all is that AJ, Brian, Howie, Kevin and Nick love entertaining you as much as you love being entertained by them. This band works hard to make every show special for every fan. With these guys, there is no "next best thing to being there." Being there is the be-all and end-all of the Backstreet Boys experience.

Karen Hoyt/ImageDirect

Brian rehearses a ballad before a show.

You are crowding into the venue with your friends and family, one of a surging mass of similarly excited fans on the verge of a happy panic at the thought of what you're about to see. Once inside, the auditorium fills up with thrilled fans whose steady rumble of cheers and applause fills your ears before the Backstreet Boys even come onto the stage. Security has been beefed up around the group just to make sure no over-excited fans keep them from starting the show on time.

You look around and see that signs of greeting and adoration are waving from all over the auditorium, and many, even you, stand ready with your camera, loaded with film to make a solid memory out of the evening.

Then there is a human thunder in the venue; the constant scream raises several decibels as the Backstreet Boys are spotlighted on the stage. The show has begun. You can feel your blood coursing through your veins.

It's been nearly 10 years since the Backstreet Boys formed in Florida, so they have almost a decade's worth of music to give you. The older European hits are mixed with the late 1990s classics flawlessly. The mix is incredible; great rock, R&B and ballads are sung with the band, unplugged or a cappella. They can do it all for a small, intimate audience or an auditorium filled across the floor and along the walls.

"Plenty of explosions, slick lights, fireworks and costume changes, not to mention 'the largest indoor concert set ever constructed,' made it all the better to see one of the world's biggest boy bands. "

— The Toronto Sun about the Black & Blue concert. ♪

If it's a small venue, the concert can be a romantic affair with the Backstreet Boys dressed in fine dark suits, giving their all to such songs as "That's What She Said," "Lay Down Beside Me," "I Need You Tonight" and "All I Have To Give."

But for the larger crowds, the concert is a genuine party with several thousand of their best friends joining in on the fun. "I'll Never Break Your Heart," "Get Down," "Quit Playin' Games (With My Heart)," "We've Got It Going On" and the energetic "Let's Have A Party" are mixed with many tunes from *Millennium* and *Black & Blue,* like "Larger Than Life," "I Want It That Way" and so many more.

No matter what or how they sing, the Backstreet Boys rule the house. They keep up a remarkably high energy level and make it look so easy to sing and dance at the same time for over an hour. They bring the energetic audience into the mix, coaxing a few bars out of the crowd. That's a nice thing about the Backstreet Boys – they don't just perform on stage and get the tunes out, they fully appreciate their fans and sing directly to them, trying to make this massive crowd an interactive part of the show, which they genuinely become during certain songs.

AP/WWP

Nick claps his hands and encourages the audience to do the same during a concert in Germany.

Another nice touch is that the Backstreet Boys are perfectly happy to split up and let each other have time alone on stage to perform solo, whether singing their own personal choices or taking a turn on their own instruments.

Touring is among the group's highest priorities, and their only thoughts are of the audience, and not the sometimes mean-spirited press that has been waiting for the group to fail since they first hit the concert stage.

AP/WWP

AJ sings his heart out to listeners at a recent Florida concert.

"When we first started out," AJ told a North Carolina radio audience, "when we released the very first Backstreet Boys album in the U.S., it was kind of inevitable [to get that kind of reaction]. I mean, we really had nowhere to go hide, you know, underneath a chair or something and just say, we're not going to take it, and this and that, and kinda run away. We always dealt with it head on and basically it's gonna happen. It still happens to this day, but it's going to continue to happen just because of our image."

Nick described a regular tour day to Yahoo fans: "There is a type A, type B and type C [day]. Type A would be a normal tour day – you sleep from 11 at night, you just did a show, and then you sleep all the way until noon, 2 or 3. You wake up, pack and get on the bus and travel to the venue, then you do it all again. Then there's type B, a promotional tour which is hell on earth – well, it can be fun too . . . but you're travelling to all different places and working all hours of the day doing photo shoots, television shoots. Then there's type C: the day off. Which you just gotta love!"

As much as the Backstreet Boys love performing for their fans, it can get quite tiring and, because of the constant moving around and basic exhaustion from singing and dancing nights on end, frustrating. But the guys handle it just fine, and in fact, seem to be getting more excited about their concerts as time goes on.

"It's been unbelievable," Howie said of their most recent tour, "because we've moved up to big domes, like the Alamo Dome, the Georgia Dome and we were in the dome in New Orleans. In Toronto we were in the baseball stadium. But I also think this tour is the most intimate in an arena, because of the way we fly out and we get so close to the fans. But to think we can fill up these domes – it's unbelievable that all these people come. And even in the cities we've already been to before, to have that much of a popular demand to come back and not only do an arena, but to move up to the domes. It's been good. During one show, we had Lionel Ritchie come up on stage – he was in town and we were working on a song with him, possibly for a future project. When he came up on stage, we could tell we had a lot of adults in the audience, because they all knew him. We went up and sang 'Easy' with him, and even the younger generation knew the song. It was cool to see that our age range in the audience is very diverse."

Michael Burr/ImageDirect

The Backstreet Boys take a break from their hectic tour schedule to perform at the 2000 Grammy Awards.

When performing in each of their shows, there is constant music of some kind. If the guys have gone backstage to change

AP/WWP

Choreography is a major part of the Backstreet Boys shows!

clothes (and maybe catch a little breath from the dancing they've just done), their backup band will play a little, then crank it up as the Backstreet Boys hit the stage again. They goof around a bit, talk directly to the audience (there's that eye contact!), sing their classics and dance to showcase the best moves there are as the audience is screaming, screaming, screaming!

Then the show is over after an incredible finale. You're too excited to be disappointed. The concert was everything you dreamed it would be, including the cool posters, T-shirts and the Backstreet Boys books you bought. Songs are crowded into your head and you're just fine with that.

It'll be so hard to go back to trying catch the Backstreet Boys on television after experiencing something like this! ♪

How Well Do You Know The Backstreet Boys?

Think you know everything there is to know about the Backstreet Boys? Test yourself (and then test your friends!) to see how many of these fun facts you knew about AJ, Brian, Howie, Kevin and Nick!

- Howie can water-ski on his knees.

- AJ's first acting gig was playing Dopey in "Snow White And The Seven Dwarves."

- Nick, Howie and AJ have done tons of television commercials.

- Nick loves his Nintendo – he won't go anywhere without it.

- Brian and Nick often fight over the Nintendo.

- Kevin played "Aladdin" at Disney World before hitting it big with the Backstreet Boys.

- Both Nick and AJ were supposed to be on TV shows for Nickelodeon.

- Brian, Kevin, and Howie used to live with each other in the same apartment (this was before Brian and Kevin got married), but they were never there, so they sold it.

- These guys just love playing sports! Their fave is basketball.

- The weirdest place they have ever performed was in a pet store. They sang over the P.A. system.

• Nick doesn't mind being the youngest in the group because he likes the attention.

• The Backstreet Boys recorded their first song in Stockholm, Sweden.

• In 1990 and 1991, Nick sang during halftime for the Tampa Bay Buccaneers football team.

• AJ still gets scared before shows. He says, "I always think I'm going to forget the words. But then the music comes up and it all comes back."

• May 8, 1993, was the first time the Backstreet Boys sang in front of an audience together (it was at Sea World).

• AJ's favorite chocolate bar is Hershey's Cookies n' Cream.

• Howie's favorite movie is *Willie Wonka And The Chocolate Factory.*

• Kevin spent eight years of his life living in a log cabin.

• Howie speaks fluent Spanish.

• Nick was the lead in his fourth grade play *Phantom Of The Opera.*

• Nick is a licensed scuba diver.

• Kevin is a qualified ballroom dance instructor.

• AJ is a skilled puppeteer.

Index

Use this index to find the individuals mentioned or pictured in this book. Pages are listed in numerical order and represent photos as well as text.

The Hottest Topics In America Today!

WHO ARE THESE PEOPLE *Anyway?*

Loaded With Fun Facts About Your Favorite People!

Makes A Great Gift!

Check Out Our Other Exciting Titles!

Movie Actors & Actresses
TV Newscasters
TV Talk Show Hosts
Radio Talk Show Hosts
Sports Superstars
Women In Sports
Influential Women
'NSYNC
The Bushes
The Bush White House

Every book is in full color and features as many as 25 close-ups of people in our daily lives.

CheckerBee Publishing • 800-746-3686 • www.CheckerBee.com